LABOR LAW HANDBOOK

LABOR LAW HANDBOOK

MICHAEL YATES

SOUTH END PRESS
BOSTON, MA

Library of Congress Cataloging in Publication Data

Yates, Michael, 1946—
    Labor law handbook.

    Includes bibliographies and indexes.
    1. Labor laws and legislation—United States.

I. Title
KF3369.Y38 1987   344.73'01   85—2273
ISBN 0—89608—262—8   347.3041
ISBN 0—89608—261—X (pbk.)

ISBN 0—89608—261—X paper
ISBN 0—89608—262—8 cloth

Cover design by Todd Jailer
Cover photos by Earl Dotter/American Labor
Typesetting and layout by the South End Press collective

South End Press 116 St. Botolph St. Boston, MA 02115

for my parents
Irene and Carl Yates

Acknowledgements

I would like to thank John Schall, Todd Jailer, and the South End Press Collective for the friendly and professional help which they gave me in preparing this book. I would also like to thank Robert Baugh for providing me with much of the material incorporated into Chapter 6: Labor Law Reform. The Special Grants Committee of the University of Pittsburgh at Johnstown awarded me a grant in the summer of 1980 to begin work on this book. I thank the Committee for its generosity. I owe a special debt of gratitude to my teacher Herbert Chesler, who first taught me about the labor movement. Finally, I want to thank Sandy Golden and Sharon Wilson for typing the final and many other versions of the manuscript.

TABLE OF CONTENTS

Chapter 1 _____

THE IMPORTANCE OF LABOR LAW

A. What Would You Do?

—Maria L. works in a small garment factory in New York City. She works at a piece rate. She figured out her average hourly wage rate and found that it was $2.50 per hour. A friend told her that this was less than the minimum wage and that she could get back pay from her employer. Is her friend right? If so, what should she do? During several weeks she also worked more than forty hours but her piece rate did not change. Is she being cheated out of overtime pay?

—Jane M. and Wiley S. are members of a union of custodians and maintenance workers at a public college. Jane does basically the same work as male custodians but gets paid less. She also never seems to get any overtime. The contract has a no discrimination clause. Jane thinks the contract is being violated. Is it? Should she file a grievance? What else can she do? Wiley S. is black and has been an assistant foreman for several years. A foreman position opens up and Wiley applies. The job is given to a young white man with no previous experience. This man's father is the only eligible person who has not joined Wiley's union. Have Wiley's rights been violated? What should he do?

—Mike K. thought that he and his coworkers needed a union, so he began to organize one. During the union campaign, Mike's shifts were continually changed. The company forced all of the workers to attend anti-union meetings. It refused to give union organizers a list of the employees' mailing addresses. Company supervisors started spying on workers at work. Is this employer doing anything illegal?

—George S. is a plant guard at Bethlehem Steel Corporation. A couple of years ago he claimed that guards were not being paid for overtime work. He also complained about working conditions. In response the company suspended George. Guards do not belong to a union, and no organizing campaign was in progress. Do they have any legal rights? What about the overtime claim?

—Lisa H. was a negotiator for the United Farm Workers Union. She was getting nowhere in bargaining with tomato grower Roger Donlon. Donlon kept coming to meetings and occasionally he presented a proposal about wages, hours, and working conditions, but it was obvious that Donlon had no intention of signing a contract. Was he violating the law? Should the union file a charge against him? What will the workers get if Donlon is found guilty of bad faith bargaining?

—Workers at McQuaide Trucking Company in Pennsylvania petitioned for a union election. But before any election could be held, McQuaide fired many union sympathizers. The union called a strike. The company then hired as many scabs as it could. If the union election had been held after the strike was called, who would have had the right to vote? The former workers? The scabs? Both?

—Steelworkers at the Robertshaw Corporation plant in Indiana, Pennsylvania have been on strike for several weeks. When they rejected the company's last contract offer, the company threatened to shut down. Is this legal? If it is and the plant closes, can the workers do anything to protect themselves?

—In 1979 some teachers at Boston University honored the picket lines of striking clerical workers at the school. After the strike, the president of the university tried to get them dismissed. What are their rights in this situation? Is it ever legal for workers to strike or boycott in sympathy with other workers?

—Shop steward and welder, Richard Ostrowski, lost his job as steward when he held a meeting on the effects of low level radiation on welders and mechanics at the Con Edison plant where he worked in Westchester, New York. The meeting was not authorized by his union, Utility Workers Local 1-2. Is there anything Ostrowski can do to regain his stewardship?

—In 1978 Duke University's 2100 hospital employees began a union organizing campaign. In response Duke hired an anti-union consultant which engineered a campaign based on rumors, threats, and intimidation to defeat the union. As one employee said,

> Supervisors told the people if they went with the union they might lose their jobs whenever someone with more seniority wanted it. They were told that the first thing the union will do is go on strike, and you'll never get another job, and you won't get unemployment, and you won't get food stamps. People were scared to death.[1]

The union lost the election. Were Duke's tactics legal? If not, what could the workers do?

*

How many of the above labor law questions can you answer? If you are a rank-and-file worker, union member or not, you probably cannot answer any of them. If you are a shop steward or a union official, maybe you can answer a couple of them. But it would be a rare person who could answer as many as half of them. There is no doubt that the questions are important. Situations like these happen every day.

The labor laws affect all workers in many ways. They influence the ability of workers to organize a union by dictating the procedures by which a union can be formed. They help to determine what happens at the bargaining table by limiting the subjects which can be discussed. They affect our choice of strategies when we confront our employers by their detailed regulation of our best weapons—strikes, picketing, boycotts, and political action. They lay down our legal rights with respect to our employers and to our unions, and they spell out how we can enforce these rights. They say things about health, safety, discrimination, wages, and hours which we can use to our advantage.

Given all this, you would think that labor laws would be well known by workers, but unfortunately this is not the case. Workers remain ignorant of the very laws which they must, for their own protection, know the most about. Ironically, it is employers who know more about labor law and understand its importance. They have formed numerous foundations and lobbying groups whose main purposes are to find loopholes in the existing labor laws and to press for repressive new legislation. They have begun to organize and to hire labor "consulting" firms whose business it is to stop unions by any means necessary including violations of the labor laws. Hundreds of millions of dollars have been spent by businesses large and small to change labor laws and to subvert them, proof positive that they are important and potentially of great value to workers.

The corporate attack upon the legal rights of workers has been very successful. It has defeated every recent attempt to reform the federal labor laws. The mild 1977 Labor Law Reform Act, for example, was the focus of massive corporate lobbying. An article in *Southern Exposure* magazine quotes one "Congressional insider" as saying:

They literally blew us out of the water. They had every
small businessman, medium-sized company and corporate
leader in the country flood us with letters. They came in
person. They came in groups. They twisted arms till there
were no arms left to twist. I've never seen lobbying like that
in my 20 years on the Hill.[2]

The anti-labor campaign has also been in large part responsible
for the slowdown in labor organizing over the past 20 years.
Unions now win only 45 percent of all union organizing elections,
the lowest since 1936 when this statistic was first tabulated, and it
is becoming much more difficult for victorious unions to bargain
first contracts. The number of union decertification elections has
steadily increased, from 239 in 1969; to 807 in 1979; to 902 in 1980;
with unions losing 75 percent of them. Trade unions today
represent less than 20 percent of the nonagricultural work force
compared to 36 percent right after World War II. Between 1979 and
1983, several large industrial unions have suffered catastrophic
declines in their membership: the United Auto Workers lost nearly
35 percent, the United Steel Workers close to 30 percent, and the
two major textile and clothing workers' unions lost 20 percent
each.[3]

B. A Book About Labor Law

One reason for the success of the employers' offensive is the
fact that so many workers know very little about the labor laws,
what they are and how they came into being. To use laws you must
have some understanding of what they are. To win better laws,
you must know how the current laws came to be written in the first
place. Management makes it a point to know the law, so just to
stay even, workers must too. Employers have devised and implemented complex strategies to prevent passage of better labor laws
and to use the current ones to their advantage. They have also
been grossly violating the labor laws, committing thousands of
unfair labor practices each year. If workers hope to eventually
obtain new and better laws, they must have strategies of their
own.

This book has been written to help workers to know, to use,
and to change the labor laws. Besides this short introductory
chapter, there are five other chapters. Chapter Two presents a
brief history of U.S. labor laws and a description of the most
important contemporary laws. In this chapter the ways in which

the laws have responded to the struggles of working people are emphasized. Throughout most of our history the legal system has encouraged the blatant and brutal repression of workers. Eventually, however, the daily struggle of workers to assert their rights forced the government to enact at least a few progressive laws. By making clear the connection between past working-class struggle and decent labor laws, Chapter Two demonstrates the need for a rebirth of class conscious rank-and-file activism as the best hope for future labor law reforms.

Chapter Three, entitled "Other Workers," focuses upon workers not covered by the basic federal labor laws, the most important group (in terms of numbers) of which is public employees. Chapter Four is called "Other Problems" and covers some special labor law problems not covered in Chapter Two. These include civil rights, so-called "management rights" (including the right to close down plants), health and safety, wages and hours, and pensions.

Chapter Five is a question-and-answer chapter. I try to answer questions which you might face in using the labor laws. The chapter is subdivided into sections which correspond to the laws and problems discussed in Chapters Two through Four. This is the longest chapter in the book and, I hope, an especially useful one. Where I cannot give complete answers to very complex questions, I refer you to readily available books and pamphlets. Also, where possible, I try to give you some idea about the enforcement of the laws. Most laws look fine on paper, but making them work for you is another matter. There will be times when even though the law is on your side, the chances of winning your case are so small that you might just let the matter drop.

Chapter Six looks at the problem of labor law reform. Better laws are badly needed, but organized labor has not been able to get them. I believe that one reason for this failure is the hesitancy of labor's leaders to actively mobilize the rank-and-file to fight for reform. This point is brought home by contrasting two labor law struggles—the unsuccessful AFL-CIO attempt to win moderate national labor law reform in 1977, and the successful rank-and-file fight to defeat a "right to work" law in Missouri in 1978. Next follows a glossary of labor law terms used in this book.

Two final notes: Where something in one of the chapters is handled more concretely in the question-and-answer chapter (Chapter Five), it is marked in parentheses with the letter "Q" followed by the question number to which it refers. For example, if an item in Chapter Two is explored more specifically in question number 4 of Chapter Five, (Q4) will appear after it. Finally, references to court cases and other source materials are marked with raised footnote numbers and described in the notes beginning on page 191.

Chapter 2 ———————————

A LOOK AT U.S. LABOR LAW

"History is bunk," said Henry Ford, and probably a lot of people agree. History as we learn it in school *is* often dry and seldom tells us anything useful. But just because *school* history is bunk does not mean that our history is. The history of the labor movement in the United States, for example, is rich with excitement and acts of boldness and heroism to match anything we are likely to see at the movies or on television. If all workers were aware of this history, they would know that the things which many of us take for granted were won by our forebears only through long, militant, and mass struggles.[1] We would also know the lessons which working people have learned through their struggles to guide us when we are faced with layoffs, plant closings, sexism, racism, government intimidation, and red-baiting.

Unfortunately, we do not know much about our labor history, and this is just what the Henry Fords of the world want. They do not want us to know that we have changed things by uniting our coworkers and fighting the owners, managers, and politicians. They want us to think that shorter hours and higher wages were given to us by benevolent employers and our legal rights granted us by kindly Presidents. Most of all they want us to believe that collective action to improve working conditions, to change laws, and to challenge the oppressive conditions under which we live are impractical and irrational, perhaps a little crazy. To counter this indoctrination, this chapter provides an historical sketch of the development of our labor laws. We will see that they have always been stacked against working people, but that when they have changed for the better, it has only been because workers have fought hard to change them.

A. Historical Background

1. Unions as Conspiracies

Workers and their organizations are granted no specific rights by the Constitution; it is silent on the legality of trade unions, strikes, picketing, boycotts, or any other type of concerted worker activities. Probably one reason for this is that workers in a modern sense made up only a small fraction of the population in 1789. Most people were small farmers or independent craftsmen; most of the people in what we would today call the working class were indentured servants or slaves. But as trade and manufacturing advanced, a lot of small proprietors were driven out of business and into the working class, where they faced low wages, speedup, and subdivision of the work. To combat these conditions, workers, usually those with craft skills because their skills gave them more power, began to form labor organizations. During the 1790s and early 1800s shoemakers, printers, tailors, carpenters, and shipwrights formed the first labor unions in the United States and conducted the first strikes to protect themselves from wage cuts and the debasement of their skills. Little effort was made by these early skilled craft unions to organize unskilled workers (mostly women in New England textile mills) or to free the slaves, failures which would hurt the labor movement for many years.

Employers claimed that the new unions were illegal conspiracies. In law, a conspiracy is a crime which occurs when two or more persons combine for the purpose of injuring a third person or the general public. For example, if two people plan to murder someone, the planning itself is a criminal conspiracy. The law of conspiracies had been developed by British judges over many centuries of settling disputes between private parties. It was not law enacted by the government and written down in a statute, but was part of what was called the "common law" or unwritten judge-made law. Since the English common law was in use in the United States before the revolution, employers said it was still applicable afterwards.

In the many trials which took place during the first half of the nineteenth century, unions were often held to be conspiracies, and forced to disband and their members levied large fines. Sometimes judges ruled that even though the union's goals might be legal, its means were illegal because they injured some third party and therefore implied that the union members had conspired to do so. For example, if workers tried to compel an employer to hire only union members or refused to work with scabs, judges declared that the union was a conspiracy because its effect was to hurt nonunion workers (and it must have planned to do so). Or if a union legally struck an employer, but the effect was to drive the employer out of business, then the union would be a conspiracy because it harmed the employer. The most sweeping declaration was made in 1835 by Judge Savage of the New York State Supreme Court who said, in effect, that unions, by their very nature, injured the public because, by pushing wages up too high, they caused a reduction in trade and commerce. Although workers could join unions, Justice Savage seemed to say that if their unions did anything, they were, in fact, illegal.

Between 1805 and 1842 there were at least twenty-one conspiracy trials, of which unions won only six. The convictions naturally hampered trade union organization. However, workers ultimately forced the courts to abandon the conspiracy doctrine because they organized to fight against it, and simply ignored it when they were strong enough to do so. The unions campaigned to win public support for their cause, placing ads in newspapers and holding mass meetings and demonstrations. They said the conspiracy law was a product of British despotism and had no place in the United States. In June 1836, more than 27,000 people demonstrated against the decision of Judge Edwards in a conspiracy case and adopted a resolution which said in part that the courts were trying to make workers into "mere tools to build up princely fortunes for men who grasp at all and produce nothing."[2] Working people also began to organize labor political parties so that workers and their allies could be elected to public office and then secure pro-labor legislation and appoint judges who were not agents of the wealthy.

This militancy eventually bore fruit. In 1842 conservative Chief Justice Shaw of the Massachusetts State Supreme Court held in the case of *Commonwealth v. Hunt*[3] that unions in and of themselves were not conspiracies, even if the achievement of their goals meant reduced profits for an employer or less trade for the community. Nor could refusal to work with scabs be itself conspiratorial. Although Judge Shaw did not say that the actions of unions could never be conspiratorial and although there were quite a few conspiracy convictions after 1842, *Commonwealth v. Hunt* was definitely a victory for labor. It showed that when working people were united and fought for what they believed in, the government could be made to respond to their needs.

2. Injunctions

Employers did not stop their attacks upon the unions just because of Judge Shaw's verdict. Throughout the nineteenth century, they developed an entire arsenal of weapons to destroy unions and keep workers powerless. State legislatures, caving in to employer pressure, enacted numerous anti-labor laws. Minnesota and Illinois passed laws in 1863 which made picketing illegal. A few states strengthened the conspiracy doctrine by putting it in statute form, making it unnecessary for companies to rely upon judicial interpretations. Two 1865 Pennsylvania laws permitted coal operators to evict striking miners from company houses and sanctioned the use of company police in company towns. During the Civil War, Northern generals occupying towns and cities issued decrees prohibiting strikes and picketing.

Workers fought against these laws through their trade unions and political organizations, sometimes with success. After the arrest and conviction of mine workers' leader John Siney for conspiracy during a long strike in 1875, labor and public protest succeeded in getting Pennsylvania's conspiracy law repealed. Labor agitation also helped to win passage of laws in a few states which specifically legalized unions. However, the owners did not have to rely solely upon legislation. They could simply fire union leaders, import strikebreakers (protected by local or state police), and blacklist "troublemakers." They often forced their employees to sign "yellow dog" contracts, by which workers agreed not to join any labor union while employed by the company, on pain of dismissal if they did. All of these methods of crushing unionism were perfectly legal; in no cases were employers ever convicted of conspiracies to injure their workers. And when several states made laws which prohibited the use of yellow dog contracts, the Supreme Court promptly declared them unconstitutional. In the famous *Hitchman Coal*[4] decision of 1917, the Supreme Court said that abolishing yellow dog contracts would violate the freedom of employers to hire whomever they pleased. It declared that a company's right to make nonmembership in a union a condition of employment was "beyond question."

The most important device employers relied upon to contain unionization after the 1880s was the labor injunction.[5] An injunction is a court order issued by an equity court (a judge but no jury) demanding that certain persons stop doing certain things which threaten injury to other people's property. For example, if there is a tree on the border between our yards and you threaten to cut it down, claiming that it's on your land, I can get an injunction stopping you from doing this until we find out on whose property the tree stands. During the 1880s, judges began to rule that "property" included the employers' "right to do business," and this opened up the use of injunctions against strikes and picketing, which obviously may infringe upon employers "right to do business." Injunctions could be issued by judges without a hearing. If a person violated an injunction, he or she could be held in contempt of court and fined or imprisoned. The contempt hearing did not involve a jury and was presided over by the same judge who issued the original injunction. It should be noted that, from a purely legal viewpoint, this was a totally unjustifiable use of injunctions.

Employers were delighted with this new weapon, especially since conspiracy charges against unions were being denied by pro-labor juries. To get an injunction an employer had only to find a friendly judge (of which there were many; in fact, in many company towns, judges were company employees). Owners streamed into state and federal courts seeking injunctions, claiming that union organizing, strikes, picketing, meetings, etc., either were causing or might cause them property loss. The judges all too eagerly agreed with them and issued injunctions, which usually were enough to break a strike or destroy a union.

The most outrageous type of injunction was the "blanket" injunction, which forbade virtually any action by any person which might conceivably aid striking workers. To crush the Pullman strike of 1894, the railroad barons obtained injunctions against union president Eugene V. Debs and other union officers. These injunctions, along with hundreds of others issued throughout the country, prohibited anyone, anywhere, at any time, from encouraging the strike or interfering with operations of the struck railroads. Debs was forbidden to communicate in any way with strikers and strike leaders across the country, except to tell them to go back to work. When the strike continued, Debs was arrested for contempt of court (and conspiracy as well) because it was presumed that, since the strike had not ended, Debs must be violating the injunction. He was convicted in 1895, a decision which, in the words of one scholar, "[put] the stamp of the nation's highest legal authority upon the doctrine that labor unions were illegal and enjoinable conspiracies in at least certain circumstances—which seemed to be when they posed a clear and present threat to the status quo."[6]

The use of injunctions in labor disputes increased in every decade from 1890 to 1930, reaching a peak during the 1920s when

921 injunctions were issued by state and federal courts. Injunctions were issued to stop picketing or severely limit it; to stop union organizing where workers had signed yellow dog contracts; to stop boycotts; to end strikes; even to prevent unions from paying strike benefits and strike supporters from operating soup kitchens for strikers. When, in the early 1900s, states made laws restricting the use of labor injunctions, the Supreme Court once again declared these laws unconstitutional.

3. Unions as Monopolies

With the passage of the Sherman Antitrust Act in 1890, capital discovered another weapon with which to attack labor. Allegedly passed to discourage the formation of business monopolies or trusts, the Sherman Act was used by employers to destroy unions instead. The Act made concerted action (conspiracy) illegal which had the effect of restraining trade among states, or, in legal jargon, restricting interstate commerce. For example, if General Motors and Ford executives met to plot the destruction of Chrysler by cutting their prices below costs, this would be a violation of the Sherman Act because the goal would be to keep Chrysler cars from being sold in interstate commerce.

In a series of decisions, issued between 1900 and 1930, the Supreme Court held that many of the normal activities of trade unions put them in violation of the Sherman Act. In the *Danbury Hatters Case* (1908),[7] the court said that a nationwide boycott initiated by the union urging wholesalers and retailers not to buy the products of a nonunion employer (Loewe and Co.) was a "restraint of trade." The Court found the union members personally liable for damages suffered by Loewe as a result of lost sales caused by the boycott and fined them collectively $285,000. Some of the workers had to sell their houses to pay the fines. In the *Bucks Stove Case* (1911),[8] the American Federation of Labor (AFL) itself was found guilty of an antitrust violation simply for printing in its newspaper a statement in support of a union boycott against the Buck's Stove and Range Company. This case demonstrated clearly that the courts considered the suppression of unions more important than freedom of the press.

These two cases along with some others effectively outlawed the use of boycotts by unions, dealing workers a serious blow because boycotts had long been a powerful and often successful tool with which to combat employers. However, the courts were not content with prohibiting boycotts; they began to hand down rulings which suggested that strikes were restraints of trade. In 1924 a lower court said in the *United Leather Workers Case*[9] that any strike which prevented the production of goods sold in interstate commerce was illegal. The Supreme Court overturned this decision, but the high court did rule in the *Coronado Case* (1925)[10] that a strike could be illegal if the strikers had consciously intended to restrict interstate commerce. It based this decision on the testimony of a former union official who claimed that the purpose of the strike was to "keep scab coal off the market."

4. The Common Law of Picketing

Nearly all strikes and boycotts involve picketing. Picketing is a basic weapon of workers; it informs the public of a labor dispute and it keeps scabs from entering a struck workplace. Without it, labor's power is greatly reduced. Not surprisingly, before the 1930s, most courts took a dim view of picketing. Picketing was within the jurisdiction of state courts, many of which held that all picketing was illegal. Workers in these states could join unions and strike their employers, but if they picketed, they were subject to injunctions and/or damage suits by their employers. By 1930, state courts generally allowed "primary" picketing, that is, picketing of an employer by its workers, as long as it was peaceful. However, "secondary" or "stranger" picketing, in which some or all of the pickets were not employees of the employer involved in the labor dispute, was strictly illegal. This meant that all picketing to support a secondary boycott and most organizational picketing (picketing, usually by union members, to force an employer to recognize the union) were prohibited. A very few state courts, most notably those of New York, sometimes held that all peaceful picketing was legal because it was a form of free speech and therefore protected by the Constitution. These state court decisions banning or restricting picketing were not based upon written state laws, although the states could regulate picketing by statute. Rather, once again, they were the results of the courts' interpretations of the "common law," law which always seemed to benefit the employers. As we will soon see, the common law was only interpreted to the advantage of workers *after* they forced the courts, through their united struggle, to recognize their power.

5. Labor's Responses

The period between the end of the Civil War and the beginning of the twentieth century was one of immense changes in the United States economy. Great fortunes were accumulated by the industrialists and financiers who were monopolizing the nation's basic industries—oil, steel, tobacco, railroads, etc. Great factories employing hundreds and even thousands of workers were built to produce the goods which were rapidly making the United States the world's largest economy. Inside these factories, work was subdivided, greatly reducing the need for skilled workers. The unskilled and semi-skilled laborers who filled the factories faced long hours, low wages, periodic unemployment, and hazardous working conditions. Many of the factory hands were rural boys unable to earn a living as farmers and recently arrived immigrants from all parts of the world. During this time, the United States was becoming a nation of big business and a nation of workers, and the lines which separated working people from their employers were growing sharper. Working people responded to the changing scene surrounding them in many ways, groping, often in a confused manner, for ways to improve their lives. Some thought that only the abolition of the wage system itself and the establishment of some type of cooperative production would ultimately improve their lot. The Knights of Labor, for example, "advanced a program aiming at the organization of the entire working class and the abolition of 'wage slavery'." The Knights saw monopoly as an evil and wanted it abolished. The way to do that, they believed, was through government ownership of the railroads, telegraphs, and telephones. Not until a cooperative society took the place of the wage system would the inevitable tendency toward monopoly be halted.[11] In the wake of the tremendous agitation for the eight hour day during the 1880s, membership in the Knights swelled to over 700,000.

The Knights soon collapsed, victims of poor leadership and faulty organizational structure among other things, and the eight hour movement of the 1880s and the nationwide strikes of 1877's "Great Upheaval" ended in immediate failure. However, all of these events and movements were ultimately beneficial to working people. First of all, workers did win some concrete victories during the post-Civil War era: some states passed favorable labor legislation, especially laws regulating safety and the labor of women and children; thousands of workers won shorter work days, some winning the cherished eight-hour day; hundreds of local and quite a few national unions were formed; and local and national federations of unions were begun. Secondly, though each surge forward by working people was usually followed by extreme repression by employers and the government, the gains which workers made and the knowledge which they acquired through struggle and hardship were never totally forgotten. The daily degradations which workers suffered made many of them hostile toward the employing classes and the government, and in the 1880s and the 1890s they flocked to the banners of the Knights of

Labor, the Socialist Labor Party, and the Populists, whose programs and actions spoke to their needs.

The Knights of Labor had many problems but their basic ideas of organizing the entire working class—regardless of skill, religion, or race—and promoting labor's interests through political action were correct.[12] Had the labor movement continued to develop along these lines, combining worker solidarity and anti-corporate politics, it might have won progressive labor legislation long before the 1930s. Tragically, this did not happen. Skilled craft workers gradually abandoned their ideals and also refused to organize unskilled workers, blacks, and women. Racism was rampant in the labor movement; most unions, notably the Railway Brotherhoods, had constitutional bans against admitting blacks as members, and only a very few labor organizations such as the United Mine Workers and the Knights actively tried to get black workers to join. The attitude of unions towards Chinese workers was also deplorable. In a speech made in St. Paul in 1905, Samuel Gompers "warned that the 'Caucasians' were not going to let their standard of living be destroyed by Negroes, Chinamen, Japanese 'or any others'."[13] Naturally, racism antagonized black and other minority workers and prevented the development of the solidarity necessary to win better labor laws and working conditions. Indeed, the present poverty of millions of blacks is testimony to the major historical failure of the labor movement, and much of labor's weakness can be attributed to it. This is not to say that the unions were totally responsible for racism. On the contrary, employers, through use of blacks as strikebreakers and through open encouragement of racism, were just as guilty. However, it has always been the labor movement which has espoused the rights of the poor and downtrodden, championed the ideal of equality, and said that "an injury to one is the concern of all." It must be stated then that the longstanding racism of significant parts of the labor movement was and is a blot upon its achievements.

The American Federation of Labor (AFL), formed in 1886 under the leadership of Samuel Gompers, developed a philosophy of "business unionism" which accepted the capitalist system as permanent and refused to consider the organization of the millions of unskilled industrial workers, or to force member unions to integrate. Instead it concentrated upon building strong craft unions to win higher wages and shorter hours for skilled workers. Politically, the AFL saw itself as a pressure group to lobby for various legal reforms and to help get pro-AFL politicians elected to office. Gompers and the AFL gave up the idea of forming a labor political party, deciding to work within the two-party system and support "labor's friends" in both the Republican and the Democratic Parties. Economically, many AFL leaders favored less reliance upon strikes (especially sympathy strikes) and boycotts and more upon bargaining with employers.

Despite the growing conservatism of the AFL leaders, the rank-and-file continued to strike and to pressure the leadership to adopt more militant political and economic stands. Such pressure was combined with radical politics both within the AFL and outside it. The Socialist Party of America, founded in 1900, grew rapidly during the decade prior to World War I. It had considerable influence and significant membership within important unions such as the Machinists and Garment Workers and ran hundreds of successful candidates in local and state elections. The Socialist Party, continuing the nineteenth century tradition of labor radicalism, believed that all workers must organize strong trade unions and must also organize politically to abolish the wage labor system.

Another radical labor organization, the Industrial Workers of the World (IWW), was formed in 1905 to organize all workers into "one big union" which would win, through massive general strikes, control by workers over their workplaces. Unlike Gompers, the IWW believed that "the working class and the employing class have nothing in common." Although the IWW never approached the AFL in size, it did organize some of the poorest industrial workers and led a number of successful and spectacular strikes, notably of silk workers in Paterson, New Jersey, and garment workers in Lawrence, Massachusetts, both in 1912.

Prodded by radicals, the AFL did lobby for progressive labor laws and made important legislative gains during the first Woodrow Wilson administration (1912-1916). Child labor, women's hours, safety, and workers' compensation laws were enacted. In 1914 Congress passed the Clayton Act, which appeared to exempt unions from antitrust prosecutions and injunction abuse.

World War I marked a turning point for the labor movement in the United States. The war began in Europe in 1914, but the U.S. did not enter it until 1917, in part because of great public hostility. President Woodrow Wilson had campaigned for reelection in 1916 with the slogan "he kept us out of war." However, strong pressure from big business coupled with a German blockade of U.S. ships pushed the country into the war on the side of Great Britain, France, and Russia in 1917. President Wilson asked for and was granted by Congress extraordinary powers to suppress civil rights and punish critics of the war. For example, the Sedition Act of 1917 made practically any criticism of the war illegal.

The Socialist Party was an outspoken critic of the war and many IWW members were also opposed to it, seeing it as a war for profits. Interestingly, the Socialist Party gained considerable electoral support because of its antiwar stand. To counteract opposition to the war, the federal government began to vigorously and brutally enforce the newly enacted "war powers" laws. However, the laws were selectively enforced, aimed almost entirely at radical war critics in the Socialist Party and the IWW. Eugene Debs was imprisoned for ten years in 1918 for making an antiwar speech. Hundreds of other radical labor leaders were routinely arrested and imprisoned for antiwar activity, which often consisted of simply holding union meetings or conducting strikes. Someone was actually sentenced to prison for twenty years for saying that the war was "a rich man's war and the U.S. is simply fighting for money."[14] The Socialist Party and the IWW were denied access to the mail. Police and government and employer-sponsored vigilantes broke up union and Party meetings and beat up hundreds of people whose only crimes were opposition to the war or radical union membership. Little distinction was made by the government, the police, and the courts between antiwar activity and radical labor actions. As historian Robert Justin Goldman makes clear, one of the basic goals of the war laws was to smash the radical labor movement.[15]

Alone among labor groups, the AFL escaped government suppression during the war despite the fact that AFL unions conducted hundreds of strikes. The reason for this was that Samuel Gompers and the AFL leadership strongly supported the war effort in a sharp break with a long history of trade union pacifism. Gompers believed that by supporting the war the AFL would get the government to help it in its struggle against business. At the same time, government harassment of the Socialists and the IWW would solidify the AFL's leadership of the labor movement. Unfortunately, Gompers went beyond simply supporting the war and actively helped the government (and thereby business) to destroy the radical labor movement. Gompers even "placed AFL men on the Justice Department payroll to act as agents and informers to help the government ferret out 'subversives'."[16]

The government rewarded the AFL for embracing the war effort. As one historian has said,

> In return for an AFL no-strike policy, by April, 1918, labor had been granted the right to organize into trade unions and bargain collectively through its elective representatives, business was barred from firing workers for union membership and activities, and the right of all workers to an eight-hour day where feasible and to a 'living wage' was recognized.

These things "marked the greatest advance unions had made so far in gaining acceptance on the American scene,"[17] but they did little for the masses of workers not in the AFL. Further, the AFL's achievements could have been far greater if it had exercised a little of the power which wartime prosperity had given it.

Proof that the AFL's cooperation with government and business was a serious error was provided soon after the war's end in November 1918. With the once-strong Left in a shambles, employers, with total cooperation from the government, turned on the AFL with a vengeance. They waged an "open shop" campaign complete with the company unions, yellow dog contracts, espionage, violence, and hundreds of injunctions. As a result, unions lost more than a million members between 1920 and 1922, over 20 percent of their membership. The courts handed down rulings uniformly and invariably hostile to the working class; a 1927 injunction literally prohibited the United Mine Workers from trying to organize more than 40,000 coal miners in West Virginia coal fields. In the face of this, the AFL grew still more conservative, hoping vainly to regain its wartime respectability. This was a disastrous policy, and AFL membership declined precipitously, from over five million in 1920 to a little over three million in 1930.

B. Contemporary Labor Laws

1. The Great Depression (1930—1940)

The U.S. economy collapsed completely between 1929 and 1932. Unemployment hit an all-time high of 25 percent in 1932. Literally millions of people were destitute, without minimal relief. The Depression all but destroyed the AFL: AFL membership fell to approximately two million in 1933, but the leadership steadfastly refused to take action, even rejecting the principle of unemployment compensation. Yet there were many people, some within the AFL itself, who knew that the AFL's philosophy was wrong and would have to be radically altered if organized labor was to survive. Especially needed was a commitment to organize into industrial unions the millions of industrial workers, many of them blacks and women, whom the AFL had for decades ignored. Leftists, including those in the Communist Party, had tried valiantly to help industrial workers to organize during the 1920s, but had usually been beaten by a combination of savage employer resistance, government repression, and internal dissension.

Ironically, the cataclysm which struck the economy during the Great Depression created conditions which allowed the labor movement to regenerate itself. Employed and unemployed workers, after recovering from the initial shock of the Depression, began to organize militantly—demonstrating, picketing, and forming unions. First the unemployed organized, fighting for relief, unemployment benefits, jobs, and the right not to be evicted from their homes. Then, in industries throughout the nation, there were spontaneous wildcat and sit down strikes. The AFL failed miserably to organize these strikes, causing a sharp split within the organization. Finally a group of union leaders, led by John L. Lewis of the United Mine Workers, broke with the AFL and formed the Congress of Industrial Organizations, or CIO. In 1935 the CIO began an all-out attempt to organize workers in the mass production industries into industrial unions. By 1940 the CIO had a foothold in the steel, auto, electrical, and many other industries.

Open socialists often led these strikes, urging workers not only to defend themselves but to see the necessity of establishing a new type of society altogether. Communists fought hard to forge unity among black and white workers and helped to ensure that the new CIO unions did not discriminate against blacks. The fact that many workers were listening sympathetically to radicals frightened employers, who were already on the defensive because most of the public blamed them for the Depression. In the face of angry workers and a hostile public, employers no longer could rely upon naked aggression to secure their profits. They had to make concessions. Labor was on the verge of winning great victories.

2. The Norris-LaGuardia Act

President Hoover was not sympathetic to the needs of factory workers and the unemployed, but Congress eventually came to understand that some of these needs would have to be met, if only to prevent greater radicalization of the masses. The first concession won by the working class from Congress was the Norris-LaGuardia Act (See Q2), passed by overwhelming majorities in both houses and signed by Hoover in 1932. Another name for this Act is the Anti-Injunction Act because its chief provisions greatly restricted the power of federal courts to issue injunctions in labor disputes.

The most important part of the Act was Section 4 which stated that:

No court of the United States shall have jurisdiction to issue any restraining order or temporary or permanent injunction in any case involving or growing out of any labor dispute to prohibit any person or persons participating or interested in any such dispute...from doing, whether singly or in concert, any of the following acts...

Following this was a list of acts for which an injunction could not be issued, except where there was clear evidence of fraud or violence: strikes, picketing, belonging to a union, paying strike benefits, urging or advising workers to strike, picket, or join a union, and publicizing a labor dispute. Other parts of the Act specifically prohibited the issuance of any blanket injunctions and made yellow dog contracts unenforceable in court. By giving a very broad definition of the words "labor dispute" (i.e. by stating that a labor dispute can involve not only one employer and one union but an employer and many unions *or* the general public) the Norris-LaGuardia Act also protected all types of boycotts from injunctions. Thus boycotts such as those in the *Danbury Hatters* and *Bucks Stove* cases would no longer be enjoinable. Virtually any attempt by a union to get a third party to stop dealing with the employer it faced was no longer subject to injunction. For example, if a carpenter's union got contractors or the public or other workers to stop buying from or working for a certain employer, these actions could not be enjoined. This provision along with the one forbidding the issuance of injunctions against any strikes were interpreted by the Supreme Court in 1941 to mean that unions were not generally subject to prosecution under the Sherman Act.[18]

The Anti-Injunction Act set forth strict procedures which must be followed before any injunction can be issued in a labor dispute. Unions, workers, or groups of workers must be notified of any impending injunction and have the right to an open hearing at which they can present and cross examine witnesses. The party seeking the injunction must have exhausted all other remedies to stop the alleged illegal activity before an injunction can be obtained. Importantly, a judge cannot issue an injunction unless it can be shown that the party seeking an injunction would suffer a greater monetary loss if the injunction were denied than would the party to be enjoined (that is, against whom the injunction is sought) if the injunction were issued. Although the Act does not specifically say so, this could be taken to mean that *even an illegal act*—for instance, a strike by public employees who are not allowed to legally strike—might not be enjoinable in the absence of fraud or violence.[19]

Please note that the Norris-LaGuardia Act says nothing about the legality of worker actions such as strikes, pickets, and boycotts. It only states that when these actions are part of a labor dispute (which, remember, the Act defines very broadly), they cannot be enjoined by a federal court. As we will see, the federal government and the states have made strikes, pickets, and boycotts themselves illegal under certain circumstances. Further, the courts today do not consider all employer/employee conflicts to be labor disputes, and so today not all such conflicts are covered by Norris-LaGuardia.

Just to demonstrate how far the Act went in limiting injunctions, consider the case of *Senn v. Tile Layers' Protective Union*[20] decided by the Supreme Court in 1937. The union, after an organizing campaign, won a contract clause with contractors which said that the contractors would do no work themselves; only their employees were permitted to lay tiles. One very small contractor, Paul Senn, agreed to recognize the union but would not agree not to work alongside of his two employees. The union picketed Senn out of business. The Supreme Court refused to grant Senn an injunction to stop the picketing, a decision unimaginable before 1932. In another case, the Court ruled that picketers do not have to be employees of anybody to be involved in a labor dispute and hence be protected by the Act.[21] Here a group of black citizens formed an organization to promote employment opportunities for blacks. They picketed a Washington, D.C. grocery store which refused to hire black clerks, urging people not to buy at the store. The Supreme Court refused to grant the owner's request for an injunction because this, too, was a labor dispute and protected by the Act.

3. The Wagner Act

Given the nature of the labor laws before 1932, the Norris-LaGuardia Act was a sweeping victory for workers. With one fell swoop it took from employers one of their most effective weapons. Employers could still get injunctions from state courts, but several states enacted their own Anti-Injunction Acts. The Supreme Court did not declare the Act constitutional until 1937,[22] weakening its initial impact. And although its impact was pro-labor and it put the federal government on record for the first time as supporting the rights of workers, its underlying philosophy was really more "laissez-faire" than pro-labor. That is, it allowed unions and employers to fight it out without legal restraints and assumed that this somehow created an equality between them. But "equality of bargaining power [is] not possible, even with complete organization of labor," when one party to the bargain "owns and controls the necessary tools for work for private gain and the other party is in the position of the outsider forced to...win the opportunity for work."[23]

Workers and unions thus saw the Norris-LaGuardia Act as a necessary but not sufficient condition for the success of their struggle against employers. It curtailed the use of injunctions and outlawed yellow dog contracts, but it did not protect workers from firings, blacklists, espionage, strikebreaking, goon squads, company unions, company policy, refusals-to-bargain, and so forth. Workers needed a positive guarantee of their right to join a labor union and bargain collectively with their employers; without one they would be little better off than before the passage of Norris-LaGuardia.

When Franklin Roosevelt took office in March 1933, the only workers who enjoyed the rights to organize and bargain collectively were railroad workers, who won them in 1926 through the Railway Labor Act (see Chapter Three for details). This law was a response to years of struggle by rail workers and especially to the massive shopmen's strike of 1922. The Railway Labor Act served as a precedent for labor spokespersons who were urging Roosevelt and Congress to propose similar legislation covering all workers. Congress responded by including Section 7A in the National Industrial Recovery Act (NIRA) of 1933.

The NIRA's purpose was to reduce the destructive (from the capitalist viewpoint) competition which had broken out among capitalists as a result of the Depression; it allowed businesses to collectively fix prices, wages, and market shares. Labor lobbyists, backed by striking and demonstrating workers, demanded that, if labor was to cooperate with the NIRA program, it be guaranteed the right to organize freely and bargain collectively. Over strenuous business opposition, labor's demands were granted; Section 7A of the NIRA stated that workers had the right to "organize and bargain collectively through representatives of their own choosing and be free from the interference, restraint or coercion of employers of labor." NIRA also said that the "codes of fair competition" which industries were allowed to establish had to include minimum wage and maximum hour provisions and eliminate child labor.

Workers responded to 7A by rushing to join unions, believing that at last they had a government which was on their side. They were soon disappointed and disillusioned. Congress had conveniently neglected to include in the NIRA any means by which 7A could be enforced, so employers simply ignored it. The Supreme Court then (1935) declared the entire Act unconstitutional. In response, workers continued to organize and strike, pressuring the government to devise a substitute for 7A. Labor's friends in Congress saw an opportunity to develop a comprehensive labor bill and some of labor's enemies, frightened by the anti-business sentiment sweeping the country, were coming to see that such a bill was a necessity. The result of this strange conjunction of forces was the passage in July 1935 of the National Labor Relations Act, better known as the Wagner Act (after its sponsor, Senator Robert Wagner).

The Wagner Act was and is the most favorable law ever won by U.S. workers. Not only did it give workers the right to organize, but it also made it possible for workers to win freedoms of speech, press, and assembly which the Constitution guaranteed to them but which employers were always free to deny. (See Q3, Q4, and Q5 for details on organizing a union.)

Sections 3, 7, 8, and 9 are the heart of the Wagner Act, which contains relatively few provisions. Section 7 states:

> Employees shall have the right to self-organize, to form, join or assist labor organizations, to bargain collectively through representatives of their own choosing and to engage in concerted activities, for the purpose of collective bargaining or other mutual aid or protection.

Section 7 protected concerted activities whether or not the workers are represented by a union. (See Q66 for the rights of nonunion workers.) Section 8 gave meaning to Section 7 by declaring that certain management practices are no longer legal; in the words of the Act, they are "unfair labor practices." (See Q6-Q18 for examples.) Section 3 established a National Labor Relations Board (NLRB) to administer and interpret the Act. The NLRB's three primary duties are to conduct union representation elections (see Q3), to determine which management acts are unfair labor practices, and to decide remedies for violations of the Act.

Four types of unfair labor practices are described in Section 8 (see Q6-Q18):

1. 8(a)(1): It is an unfair labor practice for management "to interfere with, restrain or coerce employees in the exercise of their rights under Section 7." The NLRB has interpreted this to mean that at least the following management actions violate the law:

—threatening workers with job loss or any similar loss for doing anything which Section 7 says that they can do.
—increasing wages to discourage union membership.
—using industrial espionage.
—privately interrogating workers about union membership (see Q10).
—hiring strikebreakers to engage in violence or create fear in workers.
—using the "Mohawk Valley Formula" (organizing citizen's committees, spreading false rumors, etc.) to break a strike.

2. **8(a)(2):** "Domination or interference with the formation or administration of a labor organization or contribution of financial or other support to it" are unfair labor practices. This subsection outlaws company unions set up by companies as substitutes for real labor unions (see Q13). An interesting question today is whether the many labor-management cooperation teams and so-called quality circles violate 8(a)(2). They probably do not unless it can be shown that they were established to deny Section 7 rights.

3. **8(a)(3):** A company cannot discriminate "in regard to hire or tenure of employment or any term or condition of employment to encourage or discourage membership in a labor organization." Accordingly, the NLRB has ruled that, where the intent or effect is to infringe upon workers' Section 7 rights, an employer cannot fire a worker, refuse him/her employment, assign him/her dangerous or difficult jobs, threaten to close plants, etc. (See Q14 for how to prove discrimination.)

4. **8(a)(5):** It is an unfair labor practice for an employer "to refuse to bargain collectively with the representative of his employees." Employers cannot refuse to meet regularly with unions; they cannot refuse to present counterproposals; they cannot attempt to negotiate with individual employees instead of the union; they cannot refuse to put any agreements with unions into a written and signed contract (see Q20-Q23).

Section 9 of the Wagner Act created procedures whereby workers can select a union to represent them, and declared that a union chosen by a majority of workers voting in a secret ballot election shall be the sole representative of all of the workers (see Q5, Q20). Section 10 outlined similar procedures for the filing and prosecution of unfair labor practices (see Q19).

4. Evaluation of the Wagner Act

Although the Wagner Act was a giant step forward for workers, it has weaknesses. For example, the NLRB does not have the power to enforce its remedial orders, but must get a court order to do so. This can be time-consuming and, in addition, courts have been hesitant to severely penalize an employer which refuses to obey an NLRB decree. NLRB proceedings often drag on for months; it is not uncommon for an unfair labor practice hearing to last more than a year or longer if the NLRB ruling is appealed to the federal courts.[24] Meanwhile, injured workers suffer from the employer's illegal act; that is, a worker fired for union activity usually stays fired until a decision is rendered. Furthermore, the NLRB and the courts have limited penalties to reinstatement, back pay, and orders to bargain collectively. They are not allowed to assess punitive damages, i.e. damages above those suffered by the workers and which are aimed at preventing the employer from repeating unfair labor practices.[25] Back pay awards are reduced by whatever wages a worker has earned since being dismissed illegally by an employer, and the discharged worker must actively seek other employment or face a reduced back pay award.[26] The courts have not permitted the NLRB to make an employer pay any monetary penalty for refusing to bargain, so the NLRB has confined itself to simply ordering the employer to return to the bargaining table (see Q23). All of these things encourage employers to ignore the Wagner Act. Corporate criminals like the J.P. Stevens Company have been found guilty of hundreds of labor law violations, but the fines which they have had to pay are minimal compared to the suffering which they have inflicted upon their workers.

Some critics have argued that the Wagner Act helped to defuse worker militancy and encourage union bureaucracy.[27] By fixing legal, bureaucratic procedures for establishing unions and combating unfair labor practices, the Wagner Act discouraged more direct worker action like organizing and wildcat strikes. For example, suppose an employer fires a worker who supports the union during an organizing campaign. The Wagner Act tells the union to file an unfair labor practice rather than to call a strike or set up a picket line. The unfair labor practice is decided by "experts" far removed from the workplace and usually a long time after the event occurred. Employers can use the law to force the workers to "go through channels," relying upon government and union officials rather than upon themselves. Once the law was enacted, union leaders were under heavy pressure to force their members to obey it, which often caused a split to develop between leaders and the rank-and-file.

The criticisms of the Wagner Act have some validity, but there is no doubt that the law was a positive development for the working class. It encouraged union membership and made the promotion of collective bargaining public policy and it helped to bring employers to the bargaining table. Had the working class been united and had it had a progressive political program, it could have used the Wagner Act as a tool to make a qualitative leap forward in its ongoing conflict with employers. The original NLRB interpreted the law in a manner very conducive to real equality between labor and capital.[28] Unfortunately, the house of labor was badly divided. The AFL attacked the CIO as too radical, accused the NLRB of favoritism toward the CIO, and began to make "sweetheart" deals with employers, who naturally preferred to deal with the much more conservative AFL unions. Within the CIO itself, a split arose between those who wanted to develop the CIO as an independent political force, eventually forming the basis of a true labor political party, and those who saw the CIO as a pressure group within the Democratic Party. Both divisions ultimately worked to the advantage of employers who, buoyed by World War II profits, regained their strength and within twelve years of the passage of the Wagner Act were able to have it thoroughly gutted.

Most employers had bitterly opposed the Wagner Act, and many simply refused to obey it until it was declared constitutional by the Supreme Court in a series of decisions in 1937 and 1938. After this employers began in earnest to find ways to get around the law and to press for restrictive amendments to the Act. Business groups like the National Association of Manufacturers and the Chamber of Commerce organized campaigns to discredit the Wagner Act and the NLRB. Ironically, they were sometimes helped by the AFL which claimed, without evidence, that the Act and the Board favored the CIO.

The campaign against the Wagner Act soon met with success. Conservative Congressmen and the Attorney General initiated three full-scale investigations of the NLRB, claiming that it was biased toward labor and the CIO. The results of these were to make the NLRB more cautious in its procedures. Roosevelt appointed members to the Board who rejected the original Board's radicalism. Numerous bills to amend or abolish the Wagner Act were brought before Congress between 1940 and 1947, and many states caved in to business lobbying by enacting sharply anti-union legislation during the same period. Some dozen states passed "right to work" laws which outlawed union and closed shops. Several Southern states (e.g. Texas) made laws which required all union organizers to register with the state before they could work. Many of the restrictions upon workers and unions which first arose in these state laws were to find a place in the Taft-Hartley Amendments of 1947.

5. The Taft-Hartley Amendments of 1947

Capital's crowning victory over labor came in June 1947 with the passage, by overwhelming majorities in both Houses of Congress (and over Truman's veto), of the Taft-Hartley Act. Taft-Hartley is a complex, detailed, and vaguely-written law, which both amends and adds to the Wagner Act. It is in every respect thoroughly anti-labor bill, close to the "slave labor law" which organized labor called it. Its supporters said that it merely equalized the power of business and labor, implying that unions had become too powerful because of the Wagner Act. This is an inadequate argument since the Wagner Act itself limited potential workers' power in many ways. Besides, in 1947, the majority of workers still did not belong to unions.

Taft-Hartley retained most sections of the Wagner Act, but surrounded them with restrictions and added to them a host of anti-labor amendments. Among its most important provisions are the following:

1) *The closed shop, by which an employer can hire only union members, is illegal* [Section 8(3)], even if both parties agree to it. The Landrum-Griffin Act (described below) changed this section somewhat to allow modified closed shops in the building trades.

2) *The union shop, by which all workers must join the union within some time period but need not be members when hired, is illegal* in states which have so-called "right to work" laws [Section 14(b)], which prohibit making union membership a condition of employment under *any* circumstances. Most of the twenty states which have these laws are in the South and Southwest (refer to Chapter 6 for examples), the areas in which employment today is growing rapidly. They make union organization extremely difficult. This provision is a rare example of a federal statute which allows state laws to be more restrictive, and it expresses perfectly the anti-union nature of the Act. Section 8(b) defines six *union* unfair labor practices. The Wagner Act had considered only employer unfair labor practices on the logical grounds that the Act's purpose was to protect workers. Before the Wagner Act employers had enjoyed all sorts of legal rights, and almost nothing which they did to prevent their workers from organizing was illegal. What is more, the many illegal things which employers did were almost never prosecuted. Therefore, the Wagner Act attempted to provide workers with some basic protection from the anti-union tactics which employers had routinely used for years.

However, as the political and legal climate in the United States began to shift against the labor movement during and after World War II, employers started to talk about the one-sidedness of the Wagner Act. They said that unions could commit unfair labor practices too, but such acts could not violate the Wagner Act because it contained only *employer* unfair labor practices. Of course, it was possible for a union to take actions which violated the spirit of the Wagner Act. For example, a union could use intimidation or violence to get workers to join, violating Section 7 which says that workers have the right to select representatives "of their own choosing." Or, a union might conceivably make a deal with an employer whereby the employer will discriminate against employees who do not join the union. While these examples might legitimately be condemned as unfair union practices, they were not primarily what employers had in mind. Employers talked a lot about union "goons" intimidating their workers, but such talk was just for public consumption. Capitalists hoped to get the Wagner Act modified in their favor by painting a picture of violent, radical unions interested only in their own power and willing to trample upon workers' rights to get it. But what they really had in mind was the outlawing and restricting of labor's basic organizing weapons: strikes, boycotts, and picketing. Section 8(b) goes far beyond outlawing union intimidation and strikes at the heart of union power.

Accordingly, Section 8(b) does the following:

—Prohibits unions from violating workers' Section 7 rights (e.g. by using violence, intimidation, or fraud to get workers to join a union). Section 7 itself was reworded to grant employees the right to "refrain" from collective action.

—Prohibits unions from causing an employer to violate employees' Section 7 rights.

—Outlaws sympathy strikes. That is, if carpenters strike in support of steelworkers, this is now a union unfair labor practice.

—Outlaws nearly all "secondary" boycotts. A secondary boycott is one in which a union tries to get a "third" party such as suppliers, other workers, or the general public to stop dealing with the employer which it faces. For example, if a food employees' union at an A&P urges other employees to stop making deliveries to A&P, or other employers to stop dealing with A&P, or the public to stop shopping at A&P, all these would be secondary boycotts and illegal under 8(b) (see Q37). Importantly, the Act makes no distinction between boycotts aimed at organizing workers and those aimed at supporting a strike. Supporters of Taft-Hartley argued that boycotts were intolerable because they involved innocent third parties in a labor dispute. This may be true in the former situation, for example, when a union boycotts an employer to force it to recognize the union as bargaining agent despite the union's inability to organize the employer's workers directly. But it is of dubious validity in the latter case. In an interdependent economy, any strike of necessity affects third parties, making strikes no different than boycotts. Besides, an employer is generally free to hire permanent replacements for strikers (see Q31) and continue to do business with any and all third parties.

Striking workers cannot help themselves by organizing boycotts, and other employees cannot help the strikers by refusing to handle the struck employers' products (see Q38), but the employer can legally hire strikebreakers. Such is the "equality" established by Taft-Hartley.[29]

—Jurisdictional strikes are illegal. A jurisdictional strike occurs when two unions claim the same group of workers, and one of the unions calls a strike to get the employer to recognize it rather than the other union.

—Picketing to support sympathy strikes, jurisdictional strikes, or secondary boycotts is illegal (see Q5, Q36).

—Unions cannot cause expelled members to lose their employment as long as their dues are paid, even if there is a union shop agreement. Any worker is free to defame his/her union, spy on it, be a strikebreaker, etc., without fear of losing employment through expulsion from the union (see Q40 for details).

—It is an unfair labor practice for a union to charge "excessive or discriminatory" initiation fees or dues.

Section 8(b) thus takes away from workers some of their most powerful weapons. In effect, 8(b) nullifies large parts of the Norris-LaGuardia Act because it makes illegal the very actions which that law denied injunctive relief.

4) *Employers are given broad "freedom of speech" in their relationship with their workers and unions* [Section 8(c)]. In a representation election campaign, for example, an employer can say or write anything against a union unless it is explicitly coercive or threatening to workers, or if it promises them some benefit. The NLRB has held that threatening statements are not necessarily unfair labor practices if the workers know or have good reason to believe that the employer is bluffing. The NLRB has also ruled that employers can compel workers to listen to anti-union speeches during working hours[30] (see Q11). Finally, if an employer's speech is not conclusively coercive, it cannot be used as evidence in support of other unfair labor practice charges, even if it is part of a pattern of coercive actions which are illegal.

The "free speech" proviso is a part of a broader theme of the National Labor Relations Act, namely that there should be a fairly long "campaign" before a union certification election, during which the employer should have extensive rights to try to convince the workers to vote against the union. A union certification election is seen to be just like a political election between Democrats and Republicans. This analogy is false. For one thing, the two political parties face each other as equals, but employers always have the advantage of ownership, and any hostile campaign comments can be expected to make at least some workers fearful for their jobs. Second, in a political election, the victor gets to make rules, to exercise real control. A union, however, wins only the right to represent workers in collective bargaining; the employers' ownership rights are not reduced at all.

Just because an employer has an interest in the outcome of a union representation election does not automatically confer upon it the right to actively campaign against the union. As one writer aptly put it:

> Canada, for example, has a significant interest in which party is elected to govern the United States; selection of one party rather than the other may make life considerably easier or more difficult for the Canadian government in negotiations over defense, trade, natural resources...and so on. Yet no one would argue that Canadian government agencies should therefore have a right to participate in an American election campaign in order to try to persuade United States citizens to vote for a party that would be favorable to Canadian interests.[31]

5) *Taft-Hartley once again permits the use of federal court injunctions in labor disputes, weakening the Norris-LaGuardia Act.* The NLRB must seek an injunction against a union which has violated the boycott and sympathy strike restrictions of Section 8(b)(4) and *can* seek one in jurisdictional strikes. Curiously, if an employer commits an unfair labor practice, the Board can, but does not have to, obtain a restraining order commanding the employer to stop the practice until the Board decides on its legality. To get around Norris-LaGuardia, the NLRB and the courts have held that when a union violated 8(b)(4), no "labor dispute" exists, so an injunction can be issued.

It is interesting to compare NLRB use of injunctions to prevent employer unfair labor practices and to stop union secondary actions. In the first case, the NLRB can but does not have to seek an injunction, while in the second it must seek an injunction and give priority to its investigation. Despite the fact that employers have been violating 8(a)(3) at a truly alarming rate (today, one in every twenty employees attempting to unionize will be illegally discharged for doing so), the NLRB issues one injunction for every 1700 charges of anti-union discrimination.[32]

6) *Employers are encouraged to sue unions in federal courts for alleged losses suffered as a result of illegal strikes and boycotts (Section 303) and for alleged violations of contracts (Section 301).* Section 301 makes collective bargaining agreements, for the first time, enforceable in a federal court. Before this, union contracts

were not considered to be like other contracts. Typically in a contract there is a buyer and a seller. If you contract to have a plumber put new pipes in your house and the plumber installs used pipes, you can sue the plumber for violating the contract. However, a union does not sell anything to an employer because it does not own its members. Therefore many courts had legitimately ruled that a collective bargaining agreement was not really a contract in a legal sense, and could not therefore be enforced in court. This was all changed by Taft-Hartley which declared that such agreements were legally enforceable. An employer can therefore sue a union for alleged contract violations and get an injunction to stop alleged violations until a court decides the merits of the suit.

These provisions are bad for unions because they make unions very cautious about taking actions which *might* violate a contract. Thus, employers can sue unions if workers conduct slowdowns or wildcat strikes in violation of "no strike" clauses even if it is the employer which causes these actions by itself ignoring the contract (see Q29 for a specific example). The courts have decided that such suits may be upheld in the absence of a no-strike clause when the union fails to fully utilize the contract's grievance procedure.[33] Of course, in theory unions can sue employers too, but the law really favors employers because employers usually have more time and money to go to court than do unions. In conjunction with suits against unions, employers can also seek injunctions to stop alleged contract violations. Again the courts have reasoned that a contract violation (e.g. a wildcat strike) is not a "labor dispute," and therefore not covered by Norris-LaGuardia.

7) *The President of the United States is given broad discretion to declare any major strike a "national emergency"* and then ask the Attorney General to seek an injunction from any federal court to stop the strike for an 80 day "cooling-off" period. During the 80 days the government tries to mediate the strike, and the workers must vote secretly on whether to accept the employer's last offer (Section 208). This provision is nothing more than a legal means by which the federal government can try to break strikes. "National emergency" really means "hurting profits," and as the 1977 nationwide coal strike made clear, the government will not hesitate to fabricate data to support its claim that a strike is causing harm to the public. In that strike President Carter and his "experts" claimed that the loss of coal caused by the strike was creating tremendous power shortages and massive unemployment. After the strike, nearly every serious analysis showed that the government had greatly exaggerated its claims to win public support for the injunction.

8) *Taft-Hartley compelled all union officers to sign sworn statements that they were not members of the Communist Party* [Section 9(g)]. Signing a false affidavit was punishable by fine and imprisonment, and failure to do so denied unions protection under the Act. This section amounted to a declaration of "open season" on radicals in the labor movement. It allowed employers to discriminate against unions whose officers refused to sign the oaths; it hastened the expulsion of radical unions from the CIO; and it encouraged conservative unions to rid the membership of leftists. The result was the decimation of progressive unionists, the destruction of some unions, and an active encouragement to the Cold War and McCarthyism. The Landrum-Griffin Act of 1959 (see next section) amended 9(g), but it still did not permit Communists to hold union office. However, the Supreme Court struck down the amended provision in 1965.[34] Of course, a lot of damage had already been done by then.

There are other anti-union provisions in Taft-Hartley: Unions cannot use union dues to make political contributions (Section 364). Economic strikers (those striking for higher wages, shorter hours, etc. as opposed to unfair labor practice strikers who strike because an employer has committed an unfair labor practice) were not allowed to vote in any certification elections [Section 9(c)(3)]. This gave employers an incentive to instigate an economic strike, replace the strikers with scabs, and then get the scabs to decertify the union. This section was modified by Landrum-Griffin, but employers still have occasion to use this tactic (see next section for details). If a union loses a certification election or is decertified, no new election can take place for one year, in effect denying workers their right to form a new union for one year [Section 9(c)(1)]. Before a union can terminate or seek to modify a contract, it must give the employer 60 days notice [Section 8(d)].[35] The parties must notify the Federal Mediation and Conciliation Service which may offer its services. A strike during this 60 day period results in the strikers losing their protection under the Act. Finally unions have to file voluminous financial and other data with the Department of Labor and the NLRB [Sections 9(f) and 9(g)].

One final blow to labor dealt by Taft-Hartley was that by greatly increasing the possibility of charges and suits being brought against unions and by requiring unions to submit large amounts of data to the government, the Act forced unions to spend a lot of money defending themselves. The result was less money available to organize new workers and protect those already organized.

6. Labor and Labor Law Since Taft-Hartley

Proponents of Taft-Hartley claimed that it reflected "public opinion" that labor was a growing threat to public welfare. This is untrue. What most of the non-labor public knew about the Wagner Act and labor unions it learned from the pro-employer press and from business-inspired propaganda, hardly objective sources. The unfortunate thing is that organized labor did not effectively counter capital's offensive, because it was, itself, badly divided. The AFL viciously red-baited the CIO, playing into the hands of employers, and fueling the growing and hysterical anti-leftism which marked the Cold War era. Anti-communists in the CIO began in 1946 to red-bait progressives too, ultimately using Taft-Hartley to purge socialists from the labor movement.[36]

Once the left was isolated or smashed, two things happened. First, organized labor gave its support to the government's policy of suppressing liberation movements in the rest of the world. This suppression was done in the name of "anti-communism," but its real purpose was to promote the multinational corporations which were penetrating every part of the globe. When the CIO refused to condemn the government's aggressive and brutal foreign policy, it isolated the U.S. labor movement from the world's progressive forces and its natural allies. It also was in a poor position to criticize and oppose the suppression of progressive politics and civil liberties here at home, hurting the labor movement further by allowing the anti-worker ideology of McCarthyism to go unchallenged by the one group which could have stopped it—organized labor. Second, the labor movement lost its most progressive and dynamic elements. It threw away the people who in the past had always been its best organizers and staunchest supporters. Organizing campaigns and the struggle against racism came to a halt, leaving large parts of the country open for the runaway shop movement which was about to begin.

The results of labor's fragmentation have been predictable. The AFL-CIO has not been able to take advantage of the post-World War II prosperity to extend or deepen labor's power. In fact, labor has not succeeded in having Congress repeal any of the most anti-labor parts of Taft-Hartley. Employers, while publicly praising the AFL-CIO for being so "responsible," privately continued their attack against the working class, secure in the knowledge that "responsible" labor leaders would not oppose them. Not content with Taft-Hartley, business sought legislation which would regulate the internal affairs of unions, to "protect" as much as possible union members from their unions and to encourage workers to undermine their unions and act individually rather than collectively. The philosophy underlying this goal is that unions are coercive organizations which workers would prefer to be without. Of course, no mention is made of the undemocratic nature of all business firms. The least democratic and most corrupt union is more democratic than any firm, and the level of corruption in business greatly exceeds that in the labor movement.

There is no such thing as "free speech" at the workplace unless there is also a union to enforce it. Without a union, workers throw away most of their constitutional rights when they walk through the factory gates. Yet employers had the nerve to suggest that workers must be protected from their unions, and urged Congress to legislate total regulation of union internal affairs. In the reactionary political climate of the 1950s, a climate which, it must be admitted, the labor movement helped to create, Congress was happy to comply.

7. *The Landrum-Griffin Act of 1959*

The Labor-Management Reporting and Disclosure Act of 1959, known as the Landrum-Griffin Act, continued the anti-labor bias of the labor law established in Taft-Hartley. The Act consists of seven parts or "Titles." Title 7 contains several amendments to Taft-Hartley, of which the following are the most important:

1) *The Act tightened up Taft-Hartley's prohibition of secondary boycotts* by changing the wording of Section 8(b)(4) to make illegal virtually any union action to enforce or initiate a secondary boycott which could conceivably be considered coercive (strikes, verbal threats, picketing). Section 8(3) was added to Taft-Hartley to outlaw "hot cargo" contracts in which an employer has agreed contractually with its union not to deal with another employer with which the union has a labor dispute. Certain types of such contracts are allowed, however, in the construction and clothing industries (see Q35, Q37).

2) *Economic strikers can vote in any certification or decertification election (along with their replacements, if any) if the election occurs within twelve months of the strike.* The twelve month loophole encourages employers to hold-out in a strike for a year, hire scabs in the meantime, and then have the scabs call for a decertification election. Such a strategy was successfully employed in the late 1970s by the Joseph Coors Brewery, among many others.

3) *A seventh union unfair labor practice was added to Taft-Hartley* [Section 8(b)(7)] to outlaw certain types of organizational picketing. Informational picketing to inform the public of an unfair employer is legal only if it can be shown that the effect is not

to induce any employee to refuse to handle or service the employer's product (see Q35 for an example).

The first six titles of Landrum-Griffin give the federal government unprecedented rights to interfere in the internal affairs of unions (but not businesses) and compel unions to provide the Secretary of Labor with detailed information on their bylaws, finances, elections, officers, and contracts with employers. Criminal penalties are provided for refusal or failure to comply with these regulations. Various of the Titles, but especially Title I (the so-called "Bill of Rights" for union members—with respect to their unions but not their employers) compel unions to operate openly and democratically. Union members are given the right to participate fully in their unions, to get copies of their agreements, to run freely for office, to sue their unions for any sort of violation of their rights under the Act, etc. Employers and employer front groups (see Chapter Six for examples) actively encourage workers to sue their unions, creating a climate of division and suspicion within unions which is precisely the purpose of the provision. Unions themselves must conduct regular elections, and follow certain procedures before raising dues or placing a local in trusteeship (see Q40-Q46).

While some parts of Landrum-Griffin are potentially progressive because they give rank-and-file groups leverage in their struggle against a union leadership which is corrupt and autocratic, the Act has not been enforced to help such groups. Not until the murder of Joseph Yablonski in 1969 did the Secretary of Labor overturn the blatantly fraudulent election of UMW president Tony Boyle. In general, the government will not help progressive rank-and-filers unseat their leaders no matter how much those leaders suppress their members' rights, unless the workers are very well organized, have sophisticated legal help, and are willing to assume considerable risks.

C. Concluding Remarks

There are other labor laws, and there are other important labor law problems which have not yet been discussed. We will discuss some of these in the remaining chapters of the book. It is important at this point to understand that Taft-Hartley marked a return to the repressive labor legislation of the pre-Depression years, and the return by capital to aggressive anti-unionism. It created a climate which makes it very difficult for workers to organize and develop strategies to further their class-wide interests. Its restrictive provisions have influenced all succeeding legislation, and have given employers new tools with which to beat down workers. To make matters worse, employers have learned that Taft-Hartley can be violated with impunity. Between 1950 and 1980, unfair labor practice charges against employers have increased by 700 percent, making it more difficult for unions to win certification elections, especially given the weak penalties imposed by the NLRB and the long delays in implementing them. If a union does manage to win an election, employers routinely refuse to bargain in good faith, so that by 1980, "newly unionized firms avoid a labor contract nearly half the time."[37]

Chapter 3 _____

OTHER WORKERS

Up to this point, only the labor laws which apply to employees of private businesses engaged in "interstate commerce" have been discussed. As we know, "interstate commerce" means that the employer buys from suppliers and/or sells to customers in other states. However, not all workers are engaged in interstate commerce, and therefore not all workers are covered by the Norris-LaGuardia Act and the National Labor Relations Act (Wagner Act plus Taft-Hartley Amendments). The most important group of uncovered workers is public employees, that is, those who work for local, state, or federal government agencies and a much smaller group of workers employed in "intrastate commerce," that is, by strictly local employers. This latter group is fairly insignificant since nearly all employers participate in interstate commerce to some degree. In addition there are some private workers who are in interstate commerce but who have been specifically excluded from coverage under the NLRA or denied protection by the National Labor Relations Board (NLRB). These include farm workers, domestic workers, supervisors, railroad workers, and workers in "small" firms. In this Chapter we examine first those employees in interstate commerce but denied NLRA protection; and second, those workers not in interstate commerce, especially public employees. We want to find out the legal rights, if any, of the millions of workers in these categories.

A. Workers Not Protected by the NLRA but Who Are in Interstate Commerce

1. Farmworkers

Farming today is big business, dominated by large corporate farms which own vast tracts of land and often use large and expensive machinery and equipment. Agribusiness, especially in the West, has always depended upon low wage labor, especially at harvest time, for its high profits.[1] Farmworkers have historically been among the most exploited and abused of all workers, kept in their place by police brutality, intimidation, and racism. The overwhelming majority of farmworkers are racial minorities, thereby facing a double exploitation. They are exploited because they are farmworkers and because they are a racial minority. Nearly a million farmworkers are children under sixteen; many of these are under twelve. Terrible working conditions—contaminated drinking water, no toilet facilities, filthy and dilapidated company houses, exposure to poisonous pesticides—add to the daily miseries of the people who grow and harvest our food.[2]

If anyone needs labor law protection, it is farmworkers. Yet agricultural employees were excluded from protection under the original NLRA (Wagner Act) and have remained unprotected to this day. The reason for this is simple. Farm employers have powerful political connections, especially in the South, and have used them to keep their workers excluded from the NLRA. And until recently the workers themselves were too powerless to do much about it. Since farmworkers are not protected by the NLRA, they cannot use it to organize or to defend themselves against unfair labor practices. This means that their employers can *legally* fire them or discriminate against them if they try to organize. If they do manage to unionize, their employers can legally refuse to bargain with them and can disregard any contracts which they sign with a union. This is not the case for workers covered by the NLRA. The law forces their employers to recognize and bargain with their unions once they have won an NLRB-supervised election. Farmworkers, on the other hand, can successfully organize and negotiate contracts only if they are strong enough to force employers to recognize their unions.

Through striking, picketing, and boycotting, the United Farm Workers Union (UFW) in California managed to force some employers to negotiate agreements in the early 1970s.[3] The union used some tactics which would be illegal for workers covered by

NLRA, such as sympathy strikes and secondary boycotts. (Note that when workers are not covered by the NLRA, they *may* be free legally to use the boycotts and sympathy strikes prohibited by the NLRA. However, these tactics may also be illegal and subject to injunction under various state laws, including state "common law," which is usually hostile toward labor.) But when these first contracts expired, the growers simply refused to negotiate new ones and in quite a few cases signed "sweetheart contracts" with the Teamsters Union. The Teamsters promised the employer that it would not use boycotts or enforce safety provisions won by the UFW. In return the Teamsters would get a lot of dues money. All this was done without representation elections or, for that matter, any discussions with the workers at all. It was a corrupt or "sweetheart" deal plain and simple, but the UFW was legally powerless to do anything about it.

One lesson that the UFW learned from its early organizing was that without legal protection it is nearly impossible for unskilled (and minority) workers to form effective, stable unions. To win legal protection in California, the UFW began a massive grassroots campaign for a special labor law for California's farm laborers. A combination of union persistence, strong public and labor support, and the sympathy of Governor Jerry Brown, resulted in the passage in 1975 of the California Agricultural Labor Relations Act, a law very much like the NLRA but applicable only to farmworkers in California. The union's use of this law and its willingness to mobilize its rank-and-file to fight for adequate funding and enforcement (e.g. mass picketing of administrative offices to protest long delays in ruling on unfair labor practices) have helped to make California's farmworkers the best organized and best paid in the country. However, under present conservative and pro-grower Governor Deukmejian, the Act has been inadequately enforced and the Labor Board inadequately funded. Only a fraction of the millions of dollars of back pay ordered by the Board has actually been paid.

Other states have passed farmworker labor laws, but because there are not strong union movements in these states, the laws were written to protect the employers. In Arizona, where the Goldwater family is a big grower, the law outlaws strikes during harvest time and makes it difficult for migrant workers to form unions at all. Similar provisions are in the laws of other states and will not likely change until farmworkers are strong enough to change them.[4]

2. Domestic Workers

Domestic workers (maids, chauffeurs, butlers, gardeners, etc.) are also excluded from the NLRA. But unlike at least some farm workers, they are not covered by any special state laws. Therefore, they are totally unprotected when they try to form unions; that is, they are legally exposed to firing, intimidation, blacklisting, and other forms of employer retaliation. Domestic workers are free to join unions and to strike, but the lack of legal protection, isolation at work, and sexual and racial discrimination (98 percent of domestic workers are women; 35 percent are black women) make it difficult to organize and strike effectively. Within the past few years, domestics have begun to form organizations for self-protection, such as the National Committee on Household Employment, and these may soon press for union recognition. Of course, minimum wage and hour standards can be won informally by refusal of any domestic employee to work for less. This has happened in a few places, but employers can break such arrangements any time an economic slump creates a large enough pool of desperate workers.[5]

3. Supervisors

Soon after the passage of the original NLRA (the Wagner Act) in 1935, lower-level supervisors in plants across the country began to petition the NLRB for union elections. Employers said that supervisors should not be allowed to organize because supervisors are really part of management. Supervisor unions would make it difficult for companies to discipline their workers and run their operations efficiently. Unfortunately for the companies, the Wagner Act did not specifically exclude supervisors from its protection, and the NLRB ruled that they were protected.[6] However, employers succeeded in persuading Congress to legally exclude supervisors from the NLRA in the 1947 Taft-Hartley Amendments to the Wagner Act. Today, supervisors are in the same legal position as farmworkers and domestics. They can form unions, but they can also be legally fired for doing so.

It is not always easy to say if a particular worker is a supervisor. Section 2(11) of the NLRA states:

> The term "supervisor" means any individual having authority in the interest of the employer, to hire, transfer, suspend, layoff, recall, promote, discharge, assign, reward, or discipline other employees, or responsibility to direct them, or to adjust their grievances, or effectively to recommend such action, if in connection with the foregoing the

exercise of such activity is not of a merely routine or clerical nature, but requires the use of independent judgement.

The NLRB and the courts decide in practice exactly what this means. Past decisions have ruled that dispatchers at a bus company were supervisors, but those at the cab company were not.[7] Editorial assistants at a Wichita, Kansas newspaper were declared supervisors though they had no power over other workers.[8] In a 1980 case, the Supreme Court ruled that teachers at a private college, Yeshiva University in New York City, were actually part of the management and therefore not protected by the NLRA.[9] This was an incorrect decision because clearly teachers do not run the schools or have disciplinary authority over other employees. Other private colleges are using the Yeshiva decision to refuse to recognize or bargain with teachers' unions and some public colleges are trying to have *Yeshiva* applied to state bargaining laws. This is dealing a serious blow to the growing teachers' union movement.

4. Railroad and Airline Workers

Railroad and airline employees are not covered by the NLRA, but they are not without protection. In 1926, nine years *before* the Wagner Act, Congress enacted the Railway Labor Act to give railroad workers the rights which were later extended to other workers. The rights to join unions and bargain collectively without employer interference were guaranteed; however, the law also made it difficult for railroad workers to call nationwide strikes. When the law was written, railroad employees could cripple the economy with a strike, and they had done so many times in the past. The mass strike of 1922 was one reason why Congress decided to pass the Railway Labor Act, even though it granted workers rights which the government had previously refused to consider. To help prevent railroad strikes, the Act established a National Mediation Board to mediate disputes between the union and the management and to encourage the parties to submit unresolved disputes to arbitration. In this type of arbitration, called "interest arbitration," the arbitrator decides what the terms of the contract will be. If the two sides refuse to arbitrate, the old contract remains in force for 30 days. During these 30 days, the Board may notify the President that the dispute threatens to deprive "any section of the country of essential transportation service." The President, in turn, may appoint a special commission to investigate the matter and report to the President within 30 days. Again, the union cannot strike during the investigation or for 30 days after the report is issued. Finally, after all this, the union is "free" to call a strike, but the President can, and almost certainly will, ask Congress to pass legislation either ordering the strikers back to work or forbidding them to strike in the first place. Since World War II, Congress has unfailingly done so.

Railway and airline workers do have rights far greater than those of farmworkers, domestic workers, and supervisors. But, in reality, they have lost the right to strike. Recently, in September 1982, 26,000 railroad engineers legally struck (that is, they went through all of the Railway Labor Act's delaying procedures) over a premium pay dispute, only to have Congress force them back to work. Union leadership, always very conservative, unwilling to cooperate with other unions, and not a little racist (many of the unions refused to admit blacks into white locals until the 1950s), has failed to build a rank-and-file movement capable of challenging government strikebreaking. It has never learned the lessons which Debs and the American Railway Union should have taught it. As a result, railway workers have suffered steady erosion of their work rules and job classifications, and have been powerless to resist speedups and large work force reductions.

All contracts negotiated under the Railway Labor Act must include binding arbitration of all unsettled grievances. A National Railroad Adjustment Board serves as the permanent arbitrator. If workers strike to settle grievances, employers can have the strike enjoined.[10]

The recent deregulation of the transportation industry has created jurisdictional problems for the Railway Labor Act and the National Labor Relation Act. Prior to 1980, it was very difficult for a railroad to acquire trucking operations, but this is no longer the case. If a railroad directly operates a trucking service, will the truck drivers be covered by the RLA or the NLRA (which has jurisdiction over trucking)? Also, which union will represent them, the Brotherhood of Railway and Airline Clerks (RLA) or the Teamsters (NLRA)? As of now, the Railway Labor Act takes jurisdiction over trucking operations only when the trucking service is directly connected to the rail or air services of the parent company. However, as transportation companies become more integrated, some serious problems are bound to arise.[11]

5. Employees of Small Interstate Employers

Except for the four groups of workers just discussed, the NLRA is supposed to include *all private* workers in interstate commerce. However, the NLRB (the five-person board which conducts representation elections and unfair labor practices hearings and generally interprets the Act) does not have enough staff to adequately enforce the law. To help to make up for this, it has decided to refuse to accept election or unfair labor practice petitions from workers in "small" workplaces on the grounds that these have an insignificant effect upon interstate commerce. This means that if you work for a small company, the NLRB will deny you NLRA protection (see Q48, Q49).

The NLRB has established monetary "volume of business" standards which it uses to decide whether it will take jurisdiction over an employer's workers. These standards differ according to the type of business. At present, for example, a retail business (e.g. a hardware store) must do $500,000 gross "volume of business" annually before its employees will be granted NLRA protection by the NLRB. (See Q49 for other minimum volumes of business.) If you are employed by an interstate retailer with a smaller volume, you will be denied NLRA coverage. This means that if you try to form a union, your employer can fire you, demote you, or refuse to bargain with your union without fear of being penalized by the NLRB.[12] Undoubtedly, this exclusion makes it very difficult for workers in small shops to organize.

Do workers in small interstate businesses have any legal rights? Yes, they do. A 1959 amendment to the NLRA (part of the Landrum-Griffin Act mentioned in Chapter Two) places such workers under the jurisdiction of *state* labor relations laws. Some states have labor laws patterned after the NLRA and therefore do give workers in small businesses recourse against employer abuse (Wisconsin is a good example). Unfortunately, many states have worse laws or none at all, in which case workers are well-advised to be prepared for repression. If there are no laws governing employer/employee relations, workers must rely upon the rulings of state courts which will use "common law" precedents. As we know from the last chapter, the common law at best makes union membership and strikes legal but does nothing else whatsoever to help workers. The only exception might occur in states which have anti-injunction acts. If no other state laws prohibit them, small shop employees may be free to use the secondary boycotts, sympathy strikes, and secondary picketing which are illegal under the NLRA.

If you work for a small business, you can find out if you are covered by the NLRA by calling the nearest NLRB office. If you are not covered, you can find out what laws your state has by contacting your state Department of Labor (see Q41).

B. Workers in Local or Intrastate Commerce

Companies which sell all or almost all of their products or services within the state in which they are located and buy all or almost all of their supplies within the same state are in "intrastate commerce" (see Q48). The U.S. Constitution does not give the federal government the power to regulate such commerce, so workers in intrastate businesses are not governed by the NLRA. Instead they are subject to state labor relations laws. As we just said, some states have laws similar to the NLRA but many do not. In general, workers in intrastate commerce are in exactly the same position as the workers in the small interstate shops just discussed. Since almost no businesses are purely intrastate, there really is no difference between the two groups. Ultimately, it will be up to the NLRA or the courts to decide whether you work in an intrastate or interstate shop. You can get an opinion on this by calling the nearest NLRB office or by trying to organize and then seeing what your employer does. If your employer says that the business is intrastate, the NLRB will hold a determination hearing. It should be noted that the Supreme Court has given a liberal definition of interstate commerce, so in all probability your employer is an interstate employer.[13]

C. Public Employees

Employees of local, state, and federal government agencies (firefighters, police, public school teachers, public sanitation workers, and many others) are not protected by the NLRA. In 1935 when the NLRA was enacted less than ten percent of all wage and salary workers were public employees, but today the figure is close to twenty percent. The actual number of public workers has nearly tripled since 1947 and stands now at approximately 16 million persons.

Public employees at one time enjoyed wages, working conditions, and especially job security which were often superior to those of private sector workers. But by 1960 this was no longer the case. As more and more government dollars were used to pay a rapidly expanding public work force (growing because the private economy could not provide full employment and because the alternative was another Great Depression), government agencies began to act just like private employers. Speedups, slow wage growth, unsafe working conditions, and layoffs became commonplace in public employment. In response, public workers began to organize and demand collective bargaining.[14]

Before the 1960s, federal and state governments severely restricted the rights of their employees to organize and to bargain collectively. While they could join unions, they could not legally force their employers to bargain with them. They were also absolutely forbidden to strike. During the 1960s and 1970s, public workers courageously defied the laws, striking illegally and shutting down critical public facilities. These job actions, often inspired by the civil rights movement, eventually forced state governments to pass new laws giving public workers some of the same rights as private workers. By 1984 labor unions represented 44 percent of all government employees, and 36 percent of all public employees were union members.

The labor laws for public employees are complex, but they are important because so many workers are employed by the government. The growth of public worker unions has helped to keep total union membership from falling even lower than it has. Yet more than half of all public workers remain unorganized, so it is definitely in the interest of organized labor to continue to fight for new laws for public workers to make it easier for them to organize. It is equally important to know the existing laws and how to use them. In what follows, federal government employees are discussed first and then state and local public workers.

1. Federal Public Employees

In 1983 approximately 2.7 million people worked for the federal government and roughly 60 percent of them were represented by labor unions. Until 1962 federal workers could join unions but could not force the federal government to bargain with them. Then in 1962 President Kennedy issued Executive Order 10988 which provided some basic bargaining rights. In 1969 President Nixon extended those rights with Executive Order 11491. These Orders improved the legal rights of federal workers but still greatly limited them and left enforcement to the heads of the federal agencies. This meant that, for example, the Postmaster General was responsible for enforcing the order for postal workers. In effect, then, the employer enforced the Act. In the private sector this would be like the president of General Motors enforcing the NLRA. In addition, an Executive Order is not a law and can be changed by the President without Congressional action.

Federal employees wanted stronger protection, and, led by postal workers, they got it. Two hundred thousand postal workers, mostly members of the National Association of Letter Carriers and the American Postal Workers Union, walked off their jobs in 1970. This was the first nationwide federal employee strike in history.[15] It was an illegal strike, and the government used soldiers to deliver the mail. However, the postal workers held firm, and right after the strike Congress enacted the Postal Reorganization Act, Article 12 of which gives postal workers many of the same rights as workers under the NLRA, but not the right to strike.[16] This is another example of how militancy and strong organization are the keys to labor law reform. However, if you are a public worker, you must realize that illegal strikes are risky. A strike by 5000 postal workers in 1978 to protest a new agreement resulted in the permanent firing of 200 persons.

In 1978 Congress passed the Federal Service Labor-Management and Employee Relations Law to replace the Executive Orders. This law, better known as Title VII of the Civil Service Reform Act of 1978, now governs federal employee organizing and collective bargaining. It improves the Executive Orders in several ways and unlike the Orders, it cannot be changed at the whim of the President.

The 1978 law established a Federal Labor Relations Authority (see Q44 for comparison to NLRB) to enforce it (hold elections and hear unfair labor practices, like the NLRB) and a Federal Service Impasse Panel to resolve disputes (all strikes are illegal). These boards and the President have broad authority under the law to regulate labor relations, and their decisions cannot always be appealed in federal courts. The President can deny the law's protection to a government agency's workers (say administrative secretaries at the Department of Defense) if the President believes that there is a conflict between any part of the Act and any "national security" work done by the agency. For example, in November 1982, President Reagan issued Executive Order 12391 which denied bargaining rights to 32,000 overseas civilian employees of the Department of Defense. The U.S. Army had refused to bargain with a local of the National Federation of Federal Employees in South Korea. The Army claimed that bargaining with the union would endanger national security. The union appealed to the Federal Labor Relations Authority and then to a Federal Appeals Court, both of which supported its position. Reagan then issued the order, effectively overruling the Court.[17]

The Federal Labor Relations Authority can set up bargaining units without fear of court review. It could, therefore, deny certification to a militant union on the grounds that it did not represent an appropriate unit, and the union could not appeal this ruling. The Authority can also determine which subjects are negotiable and can exclude any which it feels interfere with "effective and efficient" government. This means that any attempt by federal employees to bargain over the quantity and quality of the public services which they provide would surely be declared illegal by the Authority. Postal employees could not legally negotiate for lower postal rates or probably for a continuation of Saturday mail service.

Title VII limits workers' rights in many other ways. Most fundamentally, federal workers' unions do not bargain over wages. Section 7106 gives management a laundry list of reserved rights which are also not subject to bargaining. These include the right to determine "the mission, budget, organization, number of employees and internal security practices of the agency...to hire, assign, direct, lay off and retain employees or to suspend, remove, reduce in grade or pay or to take other disciplinary actions against employees." Management even has the right "to take whatever actions may be necessary to carry out the agency mission during emergencies." Other subjects are bargainable *only if* the management agrees to bargain over them. These include "the numbers, types, and grades of employees or positions assigned to any organizational subdivision, work project or tour of duty, or on the technology, methods and means of performing work." Further, any rules set by the government for all federal agencies are not negotiable, while those established by an agency may not be negotiable if the agency can show the Federal Labor Relations Authority (FLRA) that there is a "compelling need" for the regulation. Often when a union local presents a subject for bargaining, the agency says that there is already a rule covering it so it is not negotiable. There are literally thousands of rules for federal agencies in such laws and manuals as Title 5 of the United States Code, Title 5 of the Code of Federal Regulations, Federal Personnel Manual System, Agency Regulations, etc. Most union locals know but a tiny fraction of these regulations and may not even know where to find them. Therefore, the only way to find out if a subject is negotiable is to file an unfair labor practice against the agency or request a ruling from the FLRA which makes the final decision. Both of these are time-consuming and require that the union provide evidence that the subject is bargainable. Since many locals cannot do this, they simply take the employer's word and drop the issue.[18]

Every contract negotiated in the federal sector must contain a grievance procedure which ends in binding arbitration, but the arbitrator's ruling can be changed or reversed by the FLRA. Postal workers can bargain for the agency shop (workers in the bargaining unit do not have to join the union but everyone must pay dues), but not for a union shop (all unit members must join the union). However, all other federal workers are forbidden to negotiate agency shops. The best that they can bargain for is a maintenance of membership clause, which says that anyone who joins the union must remain a member at least until the contract expires.

Title VII specifically makes strikes, slowdowns, and picketing (if it interferes with an agency's operation) unfair labor practices, and states that an organization which strikes is not considered to be a labor organization under the law. Given the broad power of the FLRA to establish penalties and interpret the law, these provisions mean that federal workers who strike can suffer serious penalties. When the Air Traffic Controllers struck in 1981 and then refused to obey a back-to-work injunction, they were all fired, some were fined, and several were sent to prison. The union was decertified by the government (since it called a strike, it was not a union according to Title VII), and the controllers were denied future federal employment. In effect, the government destroyed the Controllers' union.

2. State and Local Employees

Federal workers face fairly uniform labor relations laws, but the same is not true of state and local government employees. First, four states have no laws dealing exclusively with public employees and four states prohibit collective bargaining. In these states, public employees enjoy only those protections which the courts have given them. Fortunately these include the right to join a union and the right to be free from discrimination by their employers for union activities.[19] If you are a public employee (including federal) you can use the U.S. Constitution as the basis for such rights. The First Amendment, for example, says that the government cannot deny us freedom of speech or assembly. But since the government does just this when it says that its own employees cannot join a union, this is unconstitutional and therefore illegal. The Fourteenth Amendment, which guarantees us "due process" at the state level and therefore prohibits many forms of government discrimination, protects public employees from employer discrimination for union activities.

In the past twenty years, more and more state and local workers have fought for and won much stronger protection than that given by the Constitution. The first state public employee law was passed in Wisconsin in 1959, and since then 41 other states and the District of Columbia have enacted some type of public worker legislation.

The state laws are anything but uniform, which makes it impossible to explain all of them in a short book. Still there are some similarities in most of the laws. Ordinarily, a law grants some or all state and local public employees the right to join unions and bargain in some manner with their employers. Most likely it also prohibits certain union and management unfair labor practices similar to those outlawed by the NLRA. It will definitely contain restrictions on unions not found in the NLRA, making it more difficult for unions to function effectively. Thirty-three states have a NLRB-type employer relations board. Here are three examples of the various laws governing public employee organizing:

First, only nine states grant at least some public employees the right to strike: Alaska, Hawaii, Idaho, Minnesota, Montana, Oregon, Pennsylvania, Vermont, and Wisconsin. Even in these states, though, the right to strike is limited. In Pennsylvania, firefighters and police are not allowed to strike at all, while other public workers must go through an elaborate and time-consuming procedure of fact-finding and mediation before they can strike. If the employer can show that the strike poses a danger to the public welfare, the employer can go to court and seek an injunction to end the strike. In Pennsylvania, an injunction has been easy to get whenever a strike has lasted more than a few weeks. In states which forbid all public employee strikes, injunctions to stop strikes are readily obtained, especially since public employees are not covered by the Norris-LaGuardia Act. Public employees who do strike illegally are subject to harsh penalties. For example, New York's law (called the Taylor Law), which covers most public employees, requires that workers forfeit twice a day's pay for each day of illegal strike activity, that striking workers be placed on one year's probation, and the union lose its dues checkoff. In 1979 striking prison guards in New York lost $126 per day for refusing to obey a court injunction ordering them back to work. Their union was fined $2,550,000 and the union's executive director was sent to jail for 30 days. After the strike was broken (by the fine and the use of the National Guard), the fine was eventually lowered to $150,000.[20] Sometimes, when public workers stick together and have public support, they can ignore injunctions and not suffer drastic penalties. In a 1976 teachers' strike in Pittsburgh, massive union and public support prevented the judge from ordering the arrest of any strikers or fines for union members after they disobeyed a back-to-work injunction. The union was fined $100,000 and its offices were padlocked, but the fines were dropped as a part of the eventual settlement. The lesson to learn from these two examples is this: if you are public workers and you are thinking about a strike, be aware of the possible penalties and be prepared to pay them. You can win a strike, including an illegal one, but unity and public support will be crucial to success.

One last point on strikes: even in states where strikes are legal, a breakdown in bargaining cannot immediately result in a legal strike. Before a strike can occur, usually a mediator must be called in to try to get the two sides to reach agreement. Sometimes a person called a fact-finder must be used to study the breakdown and make a public report with recommendations for settlement. The idea here is to delay a strike and put public pressure on one side or the other to give in. Where strikes are illegal, mediators and fact-finders are also frequently used. But if these fail to resolve the dispute, some state laws require binding arbitration, while others simply let the management have its way.

Second, public workers are invariably legally forbidden to negotiate union or agency shops. Therefore, a union which wins a representation election cannot be assured that every employee in the bargaining unit will pay dues or join the union. This weakens the union financially, prevents the union from disciplining non-members (for crossing a picket line, etc.), and promotes dissension among workers by giving employers the chance to favor non-members or hire only people who are against unions. In Michigan, where the agency shop is legal, a school board filed suit against the law on the grounds that an agency shop violates an employee's First Amendment right to freedom of association. Fortunately, the U.S. Supreme Court ruled that an agency shop is legal as long as the union uses dues money only for collective bargaining purposes.[21]

Third, in states which permit collective bargaining for public employees, the laws forbid bargaining over matters of "inherent managerial prerogative." In practice this means that public employees, many of whom provide important public services, cannot *legally* compel their employers to bargain over things which would affect the quality of public services. "Managerial prerogative clauses" usually legally deny teachers the right to bargain over the size of their classes or the textbooks used in their classes. Transit workers cannot *legally* bargain over the price of bus or subway fares, and social service workers (legal aid, social security, welfare) cannot *legally* negotiate to improve their services or how many cases they are required to handle. Such restrictions make it difficult for public employees to achieve better services for the public. The government, in effect, tries to force the unions to bargain strictly over wages and hours and then blames workers for being lazy and greedy if they win shorter hours and higher wages.

Although the laws try to force public workers to bargain only for "bread and butter" issues, it is possible, under the right circumstances, to win other demands. Teachers in Pittsburgh do bargain over class size in spite of the law (Pennsylvania's Act 195). They can do this because they are militant and strong and supported by the local labor movement. What public workers have to do is engage in political unionism—build coalitions with the public and the larger labor movement and support progressive tax and spending legislation—to expose the anti-labor, pro-management bias of the government.[22] Then when they demand that school boards lower class sizes or hospitals reduce nurses' patient loads, they can mobilize the people to back up their demands.

There are many more dimensions of state public employee labor law, but it would require a separate book to look at all of them. Not only are there fifty states to consider, but some large cities have their own laws. Usually these are not really laws but executive orders issued by the mayors. This means that a mayor can change the order to suit the needs of the moment. The mayor could decide which unions are to be recognized and what subjects are to be negotiable. Certain groups of social workers in New York City in the early 1950s could not form their own unions because Mayor Wagner had ruled that a union had to be supported by a majority of *all* social service workers in the city before the city would bargain with it.

All in all, the legal situation facing public employees is complex. There are only a few hard and fast rules (strike limits or prohibitions, limited union security, no bargaining on important issues). You may be in a state where public employers are legally forbidden to bargain with unions (North Carolina), in one where your union does not have exclusive bargaining rights even when elected by a majority of workers (California) or one which permits you only to meet and discuss with your employer but not to sign any written contracts (also California). You will undoubtedly live in a state where it is legally difficult for you to support other public employees during labor disputes. In Pennsylvania, which has one of the most liberal laws in the country, you cannot legally refuse to cross the picket lines of other striking workers. So, school custodians who do not cross the teachers' picket line can be legally fired.

If you are a state or local public employee, you are going to have to find out exactly what laws apply to you and proceed accordingly. (See Q50 for a brief summary of some of the state laws.)

Chapter 4 _____

OTHER PROBLEMS

A book about labor law naturally concentrates upon union organizing and collective bargaining laws. But workers, organized or not, have lots of other problems. Low wages, long hours, discrimination, unsafe working conditions, plant closings, unemployment, and old age are but a few of the serious problems we face. Conceivably all of these things could be (and sometimes are) dealt with through collective bargaining. However, unions represent less than a fifth of the work force in the United States, and the unions themselves have not been able to cope with many of the above difficulties. Therefore, all workers, often led by organized labor, have had to fight for laws to force employers to maintain at least minimum standards. Naturally, we have not gotten nearly the protection which we need, but we have won some important laws. In this chapter, we will see what the law has to say about a few problems which are critically important for workers: civil rights and discrimination, management rights and plant closings, health and safety, wages and hours, and pensions. Be aware at the start that the laws are at times confusing and contradictory. I have tried to clear up some of these confusions in the questions and answers in Chapter Five.

A. Civil Rights and Discrimination

1. Everybody's Civil Rights

When we think of civil rights, we normally think of racial minorities and women, those who have been denied civil rights for so long. In this section we will look primarily at the labor law as it relates to racial and sexual discrimination, but first let's say something about the labor law and civil rights in general.

Before passage of the National Labor Relations Act (NLRA), we had very few civil rights at our workplaces. The Bill of Rights of the U.S. Constitution does guarantee all of us, on paper at least, certain basic civil rights: freedom of speech, freedom of press, freedom of religion, freedom of assembly, right to privacy, and right to due process (due process basically means that the government cannot bother you unless you have the opportunity to go through a neutral court system). However, the Constitution only guarantees that the *government* cannot ordinarily interfere with our civil rights. It says nothing about *private employers.* Therefore, once you enter the workplace of a private employer, unless you belong to a very strong union, your civil rights are either nonexistent or sharply curtailed. You cannot, for example, freely criticize your employer in speech or writing (either inside of the workplace or out of it). You cannot freely assemble at your workplace. You cannot freely publicize the fact that your employer produces an unsafe product. If you do any of these things, the Constitution will not prevent your employer from firing you. Similarly, in most states, your employer can legally demand that you take a lie detector or drug test (see Q52 for details).

What has been said about civil rights in private work places does not fully apply for *public* employees. Remember, it is unconstitutional for the government to interfere with your civil rights. Therefore, if you are a public employee, the government is your employer. So, if you criticize your employer, you are criticizing the government, and you cannot ordinarily be disciplined for doing so. This does not mean that public employees can do anything at work or make any criticism of their employers. Public school teachers cannot decide to have a meeting during classroom hours and claim that this was part of their freedom of assembly. Nor can they make inflammatory speeches in the hallways if these disrupt the efficient operations of the schools. The basic rule for public workers is that, unless what they are doing interferes with their work duties or disrupts the operations of their workplace, they are free to exercise the same freedoms at work that *any citizen* can exercise outside of work. For example, the Supreme Court ordered a school board to reinstate a teacher who was fired because she told her superintendent in private that the policies of the school were racially discriminatory.[1] In another case, it ordered reinstatement for a teacher fired because he wrote a letter to a local newspaper which was highly critical of the school board.[2]

If workers had to rely only upon the Constitution to protect their civil rights at work, they would be in trouble. Fortunately, there are other laws which place some limitations upon an employer's power to deny workers their civil rights. The NLRA is one such law. Employers covered by the NLRA cannot deny your civil liberties if the purpose or result is to take away your rights under Section 7 of the Act (refer back to Chapter Two for the wording of Section 7). You are free to try to organize your fellow workers through speech, writing, and assembly at the workplace, although this cannot be done on "company time" (see Q7 and Q8). You can pass out union literature at lunch time or before and after work at a plant gate. Employers cannot keep union organizers off of their property (parking lots, private access roads, etc.) if there is no other viable way to reach the workers.[3] The Supreme Court even held that a union could distribute political literature in nonworking areas of a plant if there was a plausible connection between the literature and the legitimate goals of the union for better wages, hours, and working conditions. In this particular case, the Supreme Court said it was legal for a union to circulate a newspaper which, among other things, urged members to fight against a right to work law[4] (see Q6-Q12).

Unionizing workers can further protect their civil rights by demanding civil rights clauses in their contracts. To some extent, a good grievance procedure provides protection against arbitrary actions by an employer, but it is better to have a contract clause with specific civil rights wording. Such clauses are rare in union contracts, although teachers' union contracts are an exception. Teachers especially need "freedom of speech" protection so that they can talk with their students about "unpopular" topics (like labor's struggles!) without fear of reprisals.

2. Racial Discrimination: We Live in a Racist Country

Black and other minority workers confront something unknown to white workers—racial discrimination. The horrible and brutal racism which has infested this country from its very beginning has hurt these workers in many ways. They have much higher unemployment rates than whites. They make less money for exactly the same work. They are killed and maimed more frequently by unsafe and unhealthy working conditions. They are routinely denied job opportunities, decent housing, minimal health care, and quality education.

Black, red, yellow, and brown people learned long ago that the only way to bring an end to racism was to organize and fight against it. From the earliest days of Indian slaughter and slavery, they have waged couragerous struggles against racial exploitation. Slaves revolted; Native Americans declared war; black people organized, marched, struck, and boycotted. Progressive whites, realizing that racism is inhuman and divisive, have joined these struggles. Special recognition must be given to the abolitionists, the Knights of Labor, the Communist Party, and others who have ceaselessly agitated among whites for racial equality. It was abolitionists who helped to make the Civil War a war against slavery. It was the Knights of Labor which formed the first integrated labor unions. And it was the Communist Party which pushed the CIO to reach out to organize black industrial workers and which helped to organize the 1941 March on Washington which ended race segregation in the military. Progressive whites once again joined hands with black people during the heroic civil rights movement of the 1960s.

3. The Basic Civil Rights Laws

In response to the struggles by racial minorities and their white allies, the government has been forced to act to limit the effects of racism. At various times, this action has taken the form of civil rights laws.[5] Before going into the rights of minority workers guaranteed by these laws, it would be a good idea to list the basic laws and briefly describe each: •

1. *The U.S. Constitution (5th and 14th Amendments).* These Amendments guarantee due process by the federal government (5th) and by the state governments (14th) and equal protection under the law (5th and 14th) to *all* persons. In reality, these Amendments have not given minority workers in private workplaces much help because they do not specifically outlaw race discrimination by private employers. However the 5th and the 14th Amendments have been used to justify the use of hiring quotas for minorities by contractors doing business with the government.

2. *Civil Rights Act of 1866.* Essentially this Act gives black persons the same right to make contracts as white persons. In 1968 the Supreme Court used this law to strike down a *private* act of discrimination in a real estate transaction. Since then the Court

has ruled that this Act can be used to attack racial discrimination by *private employers*. The idea here is that the Act gives black people the same right to make employment contracts as whites. Therefore, if a private employer shows racial bias in hiring, promotion, etc., that employer is denying black workers their rights under the Act and can be sued in federal court. The Civil Rights Act of 1866 applies only to race discrimination and cannot be used by women to sue for sex discrimination.

3. *The Railway Labor Act and the National Labor Relations Act.* Neither of these Acts makes any reference to racial discrimination, but the NLRB and the courts have interpreted them to mean that certain kinds of racial discrimination are violations of the two Acts. According to the Supreme Court, unions must equally represent *all* of the workers in a bargaining unit. They violate the Acts if they give inferior representation to racial minorities. Black workers can file unfair labor practice charges against their union if they think it is not fairly representing them. Also, racial bias by an employer is an unfair labor practice when it interferes with the rights of the workers under Section 7 of the NLRB. Generally speaking, these two laws are not that useful to minority workers because the NLRB and the courts have been hesitant to use them to fight discrimination and because of the inadequacy of the penalties used.

4. *Civil Rights Act of 1964 and 1972.* These are the most important Acts to know about. They specifically outlaw all forms of employment discrimination, not only on the basis of race, but also sex, religion, and national origin. We will study these laws in some detail later in this chapter.

5. *Executive Orders.* Various Presidents have issued Executive Orders which ban discrimination by employers who have contracts with the Federal government. If you work for such an employer, you may be able to use these to stop employer discrimination (see Q54).

6. *Arbitration Rulings.* These are not laws, but they can be used by minority workers *if* they are unionized and *if* there is a "no discrimination" clause in their contract (see Q53). Minority workers can file grievances if they are discriminated against by their employer or by their union (if the union's discrimination forces the employer to violate the contract). However, arbitrators have rarely used their great powers to really deal with discrimination. They have interpreted contracts very narrowly and have refused to condemn and strike down racist contract provisions even if they violate rights guaranteed by civil laws. It is therefore probably not wise to count heavily on an arbitration ruling to end racial injustice at work.

4. Some Historical Background

For all practical purposes it was legal for private and public employers to discriminate on the basis of race until 1964 when the Civil Rights Act of 1964 was enacted. The courts refused to use, *as they could have*, the Bill of Rights, the Fourteenth Amendment, or the Civil Rights Act of 1866 to outlaw employment discrimination. Only years of struggle by black and white progressives brought about any changes. When black people threatened to march on Washington during World War II, President Roosevelt issued an Executive Order forbidding racial discrimination by employers who had government contracts (e.g. a company selling war materials to the government). President Kennedy issued a stronger Order in 1961 which compelled such contractors to actively recruit minority workers. However, these Orders are full of loopholes, are not often enforced because of strong resistance by employers and sometimes by certain construction unions, and have been narrowed considerably by the Reagan administration. The Orders do affect a large fraction of the work force (about one third), and they now also apply to women. To use them, you will have to be well-organized and ready to picket construction sites. Getting publicity is very important. The government can refuse to make contracts with employers who discriminate (see Q54 for details).

In addition to the Executive Order issued in 1941, black workers forced a few other improvements during the 1940s. As a result of suits brought by black workers under the NLRA and the Railway Labor Act, the Board and the courts did occasionally use these laws to protect racial minorities. In 1944 in the case of *Steele v. Louisville and Nashville Railroad*,[6] the Supreme Court ruled that unions certified under the Railway Labor Act must represent all workers fairly and without discrimination. A similar ruling for NLRA-certified unions was made in 1953. The penalty for unions which failed to equally represent black workers (say by refusing to process their grievances) was *possible* loss of certification or refusal to certify a new union. Workers in uncertified unions lose all protection under the Act. Denial of certification has seldom been used and even the possibility of it was abandoned by the NLRB in a 1977 decision.[7]

The *Steele* decision was a step in the right direction, but it did not get at the problem of discrimination by employers. A recent book by economist Michael Reich shows that employers do benefit from racial discrimination,[8] so employers must be an important focus of any attack against racism. This means that for minority workers to use the NLRB as a weapon, racial discrimination must be declared an *unfair labor practice*. Of course, unions must not be allowed to discriminate either, but *Steele* really did not do much here either. Furthermore, in *Steele* the Courts said that unions could exclude blacks from membership as long as they represented them fairly. But how can a union which does not let blacks join possibly represent them adequately?

Is discrimination an unfair labor practice? For unions yes, but for employers no! In 1964, in the *Hughes Tool Company*[9] case, the NLRB did say that discrimination by a union is an unfair labor practice under Section 8(b)(1) of the NLRB (this is a Taft-Hartley amendment). By discriminating, a union denies minority workers their right to be represented by a union of their own choosing and their right to join together to protect themselves. These rights are guaranteed by Section 7 of the NLRB, and 8(b)(1) states that a union cannot interfere with workers' exercise of them.

So, you can file an unfair labor practice against your union. But the NLRB and the courts have never found employers guilty of unfair labor practices because of racism. This makes the NLRB a weak tool to use in the struggle against discrimination, and I cannot recommend that you use it. In fact, to use the Act at all in discrimination cases, minority workers must go through their unions and not act on their own. Independent action by minority unionists is *not* protected by the NLRB according to the courts.[10] For example, black auto workers in Detroit formed separate organizations in the 1960s to fight for better treatment from both employers and the United Auto Workers. They staged wildcat strikes and protests to force companies and the union to meet their demands for more black shop stewards, better safety conditions, etc. A good case can be made that such actions are protected under Section 7 of the NLRA which guarantees workers the right to organize to protect themselves. However, once you are in a union, you must use it and not act on your own to protect yourself.

One final point on the NLRA: most minority workers are not in unions. Therefore, they cannot use the NLRA at all to fight discrimination by their employers.

5. The Civil Rights Acts of 1964 and 1972

The employment rights of minorities took a large step forward with the Civil Rights Acts of 1964 and 1972. These Acts, the direct result of the civil rights movement of the 1950s and the 1960s, give minority workers a much better legal vehicle to fight discrimination than the NLRA. Since their passage, the courts have also begun to enforce the Civil Rights Act of 1866 mentioned earlier.

Title VII of the Act (a "Title" is simply a section of the Act) contains this important statement:

It shall be an unlawful employment practice for an employer:

(1) To fail or refuse to hire or to discharge any individual, or otherwise to discriminate against any individual with respect to his [sic] compensation, terms, conditions, or privileges of employment, because of such individual's race, color, religion, sex, or national origin.

(2) To limit, segregate, or classify his [sic] employees or applicants for employment in any way which would deprive or tend to deprive any individual of employment opportunities or otherwise adversely affect his [sic] status as an employee because of such individual's race, color, religion, sex, or national origin.

Section 703(c) provides that unions cannot discriminate either. Section 705 establishes an Equal Employment Opportunity Commission (EEOC) which receives charges of discrimination from employees, investigates them, and tries to conciliate them. If conciliation fails, the EEOC can bring suit against the employer (or labor union) in federal court, but it does not have to. An employee, however, is free to go into court regardless of the EEOC's actions. The EEOC can itself initiate investigations and suits on behalf of workers. Where the employer is a governmental unit or agency, the EEOC can refer a case to the Attorney General for appropriate action (see Q55).

What kinds of employer (or union) conduct are discriminatory? And what kinds of remedies are to be used to end discrimination? The EEOC and the Courts have made various rulings. (See Q56 for additional material.) Some types of discrimination clearly violate the law, for example, segregated union locals or job advertisements which say that blacks need not apply. However, the Courts have moved cautiously to outlaw less obvious forms of discrimination. In *Griggs v. Duke Power Company* (1971),[11] the Supreme Court ruled that almost any job criteria (high school diplomas, minimum test scores, etc.) which exclude proportionately more blacks (or any other group protected by Title VII) are illegal unless clearly related to job performance. Although the *Griggs* decision has since been watered down, it does put the burden of proof on employers to show that job qualifications are indeed job related, and this is not always easy to do. Also, with *Griggs* the employer's intent to discriminate does not have to be proven, only the "disparate [that is, different] impact" upon the group of employees.

In *McDonnel Douglas Corporation v. Green*[12] the Supreme Court declared that "disparate treatment" can be illegal. Here a minority employee who qualifies for a job but is rejected can sue the employer and force the employer to justify its decision when certain conditions are met. These conditions are that after a qualified minority employee was rejected, the employer continued to seek applicants. If this can be shown, then the employer must provide a nondiscriminatory justification for turning down the applicant. However, then it is up to the employee to show the reason given is a subterfuge, which, given the increasing sophistication of employers, may be very difficult to do.

Minority workers have long been victimized by discriminatory seniority rules in collective bargaining contracts. These provisions lock such workers into low-paying, dead-end jobs by forcing them in effect to lose all seniority accumulated in a department when they transfer out of it. Black steel workers, for example, would hesitate to try to transfer out of the foundry department into a cleaner, higher-paying department because they could not carry their plant (foundry) seniority with them. In a recession, they would be laid off first because less senior white workers had more departmental seniority. Now obviously it was employer and white worker racism which put racial minorities in the lousiest jobs in the first place, and the seniority system clearly perpetuated the racism. Therefore, the seniority systems must be illegal. Right? Several federal Courts of Appeal thought so, but the Supreme Court in *International Brotherhood of Teamsters v. United States*[13] disagreed. In this case, local delivery truck drivers (mostly black) who transferred to more lucrative long-distance driving jobs (mostly white) lost all of their seniority. The EEOC, the Federal District Court, and the Federal Appeals Court had all ruled that the seniority agreement was discriminatory and ordered appropriate relief. The Supreme Court overturned these decisions by ruling that there was no "intent" to discriminate and therefore the clause was protected by Section 703(h) of Title VII which says that an employer can apply different employment standards "pursuant to a bona fide seniority...system...provided that such differences were not the result of intention to discriminate." In other words, unless a seniority clause is blatantly racist, it does not violate the law, even if it perpetuates discrimination.

Congress gave the Courts wide powers in Title VII to fashion remedies to end discrimination. Some of these are:

1) *Injunctions*, requested by an individual or the Attorney General, ordering an employer to stop any discriminatory acts. Injunctions can be issued before a discrimination case is actually heard, if you can show that the employer appears to have a history of discrimination.

2) *Affirmative Actions*, aimed, as allowed by the law, at achieving a future environment free of discrimination. Typical

affirmative actions are the abolition of departmental seniority systems (but not to the extent that white workers are actually displaced); hiring quotas and timetables (for example, one minority must be hired for every two whites until a certain fraction of the work force consists of minority workers); elimination of age limits for apprentices so that persons discriminated against in the past can still become craftspersons; special training programs for minorities; merger of segregated union locals; and mandatory advertisement in minority communities of job opportunities or apprenticeships by employers or unions.

The Reagan administration has systematically and insistently attacked affirmative action in an attempt to roll back the gains made by black people since the civil rights movement. It argues that any affirmative action which "favors" blacks over whites discriminates against whites, ignoring the obvious fact that past discrimination, which has favored whites to an extraordinary degree, cannot be overcome unless strong affirmative actions are taken. It further says that the only outcomes which are discriminatory are those which are the result of intentional action. Therefore the use of statistics to show disparate impact (for example, that while blacks comprise thirty percent of a city's population, only two percent of the firefighters are black) is inappropriate. Even supposing that intent to discriminate can be proven, this administration contends that only identifiable victims can be compensated for discrimination. Class action suits, in which all black workers in a company file a suit charging discrimination, would not be allowed unless each and every member of the class can prove that the employer explicitly and intentionally discriminated against him or her.

Taken literally, Reagan's interpretation of the civil rights laws would result in almost no one winning a civil rights case. So far, the Supreme Court, despite its right tilt, has refused to endorse this racist interpretation, although it has narrowed the scope of affirmative action. In recent cases, it has ruled that plans, whether voluntary, consent decrees, or court-ordered, which result in senior white workers being laid off before less senior minority employees, are not legal. However, plans which give preference to minorities in terms of hiring and promotion are still legal. In one case, the court approved a plan which reserved nearly half of all promotions in Cleveland's fire department for qualified minority applicants. In another, it upheld a lower court order that a New York-New Jersey sheet metal workers' union must double its nonwhite membership to 29.3 percent by August 1987.[14] It is possible, even likely, that these rulings will be overturned now that the utterly reactionary William Rehnquist has became Chief Justice, and especially if Reagan gets to appoint another justice. Further, it is certain that the lower courts, staffed by Reagan appointees with ideologies hostile to civil rights, will make fewer progressive civil rights decisions.

3) *Back Pay*, to compensate those harmed by past and present discrimination. Persons awarded back pay need not have been parties to the original suit.

4) *Front Pay*, to compensate those who may not be able to take immediate advantage of the ending of discriminatory practices. A black or female worker might gain more seniority by a court's ruling, but might have to wait to get the job due him or her until incumbent whites quit or retire. Had there been no discrimination to begin with, the minority worker might have had the job long ago. In a front pay award, the affected worker might get paid at a higher rate even though his or her job does not immediately change. Or, black workers laid off because of past discrimination have to be recalled but white workers are not to be displaced.

5) *Punitive Damages*, to deter future discrimination and to help to repay minority workers for the terrible violations of their rights which discrimination has caused.

6) *Attorney's Fees* (what you have to pay your lawyer), to prevent such fees from diluting the award made to employees and to encourage lawyers to take civil rights cases.

All of these remedies involve complex legal questions better left to lawyers. For our purposes, though, four points can be made. First, the law encourages the parties to a suit to conciliate or try to work things out without a trial. This often spells trouble for workers. The EEOC has a huge backlog of cases. The government really does not want to step too hard on corporate toes. The result is often that the government cooks up a deal which becomes the basis for a "consent decree" in which a defendant agrees to stop discriminating and take certain remedial actions. Employees are then pressured to accept the decree as the best they can get. If they do accept, they waive their rights to sue the employer or union themselves. Since going to court as a private citizen is expensive, many workers will agree to the decree. Numerous consent decrees have been devised since Title VII was passed, including a famous one in the steel industry. Black steelworkers suing both the companies and the union were for all practical purposes forced to accept a consent decree which did not come close to compensating them for past discrimination.

Second, court orders must be enforced to be effective. Enforcement of the civil rights laws has been weak, especially of affirmative action programs. A look at the racial and sexual composition of many work forces today as compared with 1964 hardly indicates rigorous enforcement of the many court-ordered remedies issued. Third, remedies which do or could provide minorities and women with more jobs have been denounced as unconstitutional "reverse discrimination." In the *Bakke* case,[15] the Supreme Court struck down a program at the University of California which allotted a specific number of medical school admissions to minorities. The courts have so far hesitated to apply *Bakke* to employment programs. In the *Weber* decision[16] (see Q57 for details), for example, the Supreme Court approved a voluntary company training program for minorities. But, as stated above, the Reagan administration is doing its best to cripple the civil rights laws by appointing persons opposed to affirmative action to the EEOC, by watering down the Executive Orders (for example, employers with federal contracts no longer have to apply racial and sexual hiring quotas to each job site but only to their overall operations), and by causing minorities to be laid off because of the recession which the Reagan government caused.

Fourth, civil rights cases often drag on for years. Employers can delay hearings in many ways. They can force civil rights lawyers to sue to get necessary information which only the employers can provide. Their lawyers can compel plaintiffs to spend long hours answering questions about a case. And although civil rights lawyers may work on a contingency basis (i.e. they get paid only if you win your case) and may win attorney's fees from the employer, they still have to pay all costs of a case while it is being pursued. A case which lasts any length of time will cost thousands of dollars. Not many lawyers can or will carry such costs, especially since the case may be lost and no fee collected at all. Employers' lawyers know this and therefore intentionally try to delay as much as possible. The upshot is that it is becoming more difficult just to get a lawyer to take a civil rights case.[17]

Despite all of the problems with the Civil Rights Acts, we are better off with them than without them. What is needed is constant pressure on the government and the courts to enforce and extend the laws. Civil rights groups, progressive unions, individuals, and other organizations worked long and hard, contributing money, filing legal briefs, writing articles, and demonstrating in the streets to let the Supreme Court know that they would not tolerate a bad decision in the Weber case. Especially now with the racist and reactionary Reagan administration in power, such organization is crucial just to make sure that we do not go too far backwards. We should also struggle in whatever ways we can to get full employment legislation passed. When unemployment is high, minorities are hurt the most, and it is hardest to win the support of white workers for racial equality. In a real sense, full employment laws would be powerful civil rights laws too.

6. Sexual Discrimination: Women Workers Have a "Double Day"

Just about everything said about racial discrimination could also be said about discrimination against women. Women make up nearly half of the paid labor force, yet they are stuck in stereotyped, low-paying jobs. Only sexism can account for the vast differences in the percentages shown in the following table. And besides job discrimination, women often work a "double day," taking care of a household after they get home from work.

Women As A Percentage of Total Employees In Selected Occupations, 1978

Occupation	% of Women
Selected Professions	
Lawyers	9.0
Physicians	11.0
Engineers	3.0
College Teachers	34.0
Selected "Female" Occupations	
Registered Nurses	97.0
Clerical Workers	80.0
Sales Clerks, retail	72.0
Private Household Workers	98.0
Sewers and Stitchers	95.0
Selected "Male" Occupations	
Automobile Mechanic	0.6
Tool and Die Makers	1.1
Carpenters	1.0
All Occupations	41.0

Source: Ruth Milkman, "Organizing the Sexual Division of Labor: Historical Perspective on 'Women's Work' and the American Labor Movement," **Socialist Review**, Vol. 10, No. 1 (Jan.-Feb., 1980), p. 96.

Women, like minorities, have never simply accepted their exploitation, but have constantly fought for equality with men. Like racial minorities, women have also won legal victories. All of the laws outlined in the section above, except the Civil Rights Act of 1866, can be used by women to battle employment discrimination. At present, the Civil Rights Acts of 1964 and 1972 are the most important; but if the Equal Rights Amendment becomes law, it will be very important too. A law which applies only for women is the Equal Pay Act of 1963 (to be discussed later in this chapter) which guarantees "equal pay for equal work." Many states have "equal pay" laws which can be used by women in intrastate commerce. However, these laws cannot be used by public workers because they are not covered. A very recent Supreme Court decision permits use of the Civil Rights Act of 1964 to win equal pay, and this law can be used by both private and public employees.

7. The Civil Rights Acts of 1964 and 1972

In interpreting Title VII of the Act of 1964, the courts have struck down so-called "state protective laws" passed supposedly to protect women by restricting their hours of work, the types of jobs they could do, and so forth. Employers cannot set special standards for women unless they can show that sex is a "bonafide occupational qualification." The Supreme Court has ruled that height and weight requirements for prison guards were illegal because they discriminated against women and were not job-related. At the same time it approved a requirement that guards in maximum security prisons had to be men. In a questionable decision, *General Electric Company v. Gilbert* (1976),[18] the Supreme Court held that an inclusive employee disability plan could exclude pregnancy-related disabilities. That is, if an employee's disability was due to pregnancy, she was not entitled to payments under the disability plan. This was a bad decision because only women can be pregnant, and a rule which excludes pregnancy-related disability clearly discriminates against women. Happily, Congress overturned *Gilbert* in 1978 by amending Title VII to explicitly forbid discrimination against pregnant women. (See Q58 for more on the rights of pregnant workers.)

What about sexual harassment at the workplace? Probably a majority of women workers have suffered this terrible abuse. Many women suffer sexual harassment silently out of fear of losing their jobs, and because it has been hard for women to do anything about it. Very few charges of sexual harassment have been upheld in court, in part because most judges are men and

believe that women "ask for it." Women have been demanding
that sexual harassment be made illegal under Title VII, but not
until 1980 did the Equal Employment Opportunity Commission
establish guidelines which make sexual harassment a discriminating act and therefore a violation of Title VII. Several lower courts
have also held sexual harassment to be a violation of the Civil
Rights Acts, one holding that sexual harassment in and of itself
was discriminatory whether or not a female employee has actually
suffered job loss or other monetary losses as a result.[19] (For more
detailed information about sexual harassment at work and what
to do about it, see Q59.)

8. Equal Pay for Equal Work

Women have won a number of suits under the provisions of the
Equal Pay Act (this Act is an amendment to the Fair Labor
Standards Act discussed later in this chapter). Some important
victories have been won against banks, which are notoriously
sexist. A national group called Working Women has won suits
against Continental Bank and CNA Insurance in Chicago.
Another group, Women Office Workers, forced Chase Manhattan
Bank to pay $2 million to its women clerical workers (see Q59). In
all of these, equal pay for equal work was narrowly defined. To get
equal pay, you had to be doing pretty much the same job as a man.
But in a 1981 ruling, the Supreme Court took a broader view and
said that the work does not have to be the same but only *equivalent*
to the man's job in terms of job characteristics. In the actual case,
female prison guards in Oregon argued that they were being
discriminated against because they were paid less than male
guards. The women admitted that they did different work—
women did clerical work and men supervised male prisoners—but
they argued that their work was equivalent. The Supreme Court
agreed but said that cases such as this must be brought under the
Civil Rights Act of 1964 rather than the Equal Pay Act.[20]

The Oregon prison guard decision may open the way for a still
more liberal interpretation of the law. Because of past discrimination, few women are truck drivers, while 99 percent of all secretaries are women. What if it could be shown that secretarial work
is as difficult as truck driving? Then shouldn't secretaries get as
much money as truck drivers, especially when they work for the
same employer? In what could have become a landmark decision,
a Federal District Court in the State of Washington answered this
question affirmatively. In the case of *AFSCME v. Washington*,[21]
the judge ruled that female public employees were consistently
paid less than men even though the women's (different) jobs had

the same aptitude, skill, and training requirements as those of the male workers. For example, the state gave a 97 point job evaluation to both laundry workers (mostly female) and truck drivers (mostly male), but paid the laundry workers 71 percent as much as the drivers. The union, the American Federation of State, County and Municipal Employees, had previously gotten the state to commission a study which showed that women received about 20 percent less wages for jobs of "comparable worth." The state then agreed to implement a plan to close this wage gap over a ten year period but allocated only $1.5 million dollars for the program. AFSCME, dissatisfied with a plan which it argued would take 85 years to equalize wages, then filed suit in federal court, charging that the state had violated the 1964 Civil Rights Act. The judge agreed and demanded that the salaries of 15,000 workers in predominantly female categories be raised immediately, which could have cost the state close to $1 billion.

This case was overturned in an Appeals Court in 1985.[22] In the meantime, however, it served as a rallying point for similar cases in other states, and has caused several states to review their wage policies. To date, seven states (Idaho, Iowa, Minnesota, New Mexico, South Dakota, Washington, and Wisconsin) have implemented comparable worth programs. Minnesota's law requires local governments to adopt pay equality plans as well.

9. Age Discrimination

The Civil Rights Act of 1964 established an advisory council to study employment discrimination and make yearly recommendations to Congress and the President. In 1965, the council documented for Congress widespread discrimination based upon age. In response to this report and to pressure from such organizations as the Grey Panthers, Congress passed the Age Discrimination in Employment Act (ADEA) in 1967. Originally, ADEA was to use the enforcement procedures of the Fair Labor Standards Act (see Section E of this chapter), but in 1979 President Carter ordered that ADEA would be enforced by the Equal Employment Opportunity Commission, which, as we know, enforces the Civil Rights Act[23] (see Q55).

The Age Discrimination in Employment Act prohibits employers from discriminating against persons "who are at least 40 years of age but less than 70 years of age" in such things as "hiring, firing, pay, and terms, conditions, or privileges of employment." Successful plaintiffs can win reinstatement, promotion, back pay, and double damages if their employers willfully violate the law. The Act originally forbade mandatory retirement at less than 70 years of age, outlawed seniority systems or benefit plans which provide for involuntary retirement before age 70, and nullified mandatory retirement at 70 for federal government employees.[24] Recent amendments have abolished nearly all mandatory retirement ages.

In terms of enforcement, ADEA is nearly identical to the Civil Rights Acts, so what was said above in connection with them applies to ADEA as well (see Q55 also). One problem with enforcement is that under Section 633(b) of the Act, a person alleging age discrimination who lives in a "deferral state" must file charges with both the EEOC and the appropriate state agency. A "deferral state" is "a State which has a law prohibiting discrimination in employment because of age and establishing or authorizing a State authority to grant or seek relief." If you live in a deferral state, you have 300 days after the discrimination has occurred to file a charge; in a non-deferral state, you have 180 days to file a complaint with the EEOC. Unfortunately, the courts have ruled that many states which appear to be deferral states are not in fact such states. As a result, many complaints filed after 180 days have been thrown out of court because they are not timely. For example, suppose you file a complaint with the Pennsylvania Human Relations Commission 195 days after your employer has discriminated against you. You believe that Pennsylvania's law is exactly the same as the ADEA and that it is a deferral state. If the court rules otherwise, then your case will be dismissed because you have missed the 180 day EEOC deadline required in non-deferral states. The entire ADEA filing procedure is complicated so you will definitely need a skilled attorney. *Always* file your complaints in a timely manner so you won't be among the 50 percent of all ADEA filers whose suits have been dismissed on procedural grounds.

The Age Discrimination in Employment Act does permit employers to use age as a bonafide occupational qualification, and the standards for doing so are not as strict as they are for sex discrimination. To use age as a bonafide occupational qualification, the federal courts have said that it must be shown that:

> ...the employer has reasonable cause [some factual basis] for believing that all or substantially all persons within the group discriminated against [those at least 40 but less than 70 years of age] would be unable to effectively and safely perform the job or that it would be impractical to deal with persons within the protected group on an individual basis. Employers must also show that the BFOQ [bona fide occupational qualification] is reasonably necessary to the essence of the employer's business.

Employers have been most successful in arguing that it is unsafe to use older workers in certain jobs. Thus, the use of maximum hiring ages for airline pilots and mandatory retirement ages for fire fighters and police have been upheld. However, the courts have generally not allowed an ageist argument based upon profitability to stand.

B. Management Rights and Plant Closings

Management rights are those "rights" which employers claim they must have to operate their businesses efficiently. Before unions became strong, these rights were pretty much absolute. Employers could do whatever they wanted with their property, which included the labor of their workers. Workers could be fired, transferred, denied promotions, demoted, or have their pay cut arbitrarily without being able to legally protest. With a union present, management's rights are reduced considerably but by no means eliminated. Prior to the Wagner Act employers could refuse to live up to the terms of union contracts and could only be made to do so if the unions were strong enough to force them. After the Wagner Act (or NLRA) the situation changed. Employers have to bargain in good faith with an elected union. In the process of bargaining, management can lose some things which were previously its "right" to do. The question is: What must an employer bargain about? How much protection from management can workers *legally* demand to bargain over? In what follows we are always talking about private employees. Public workers, as we have seen, are legally less free to bargain than are private employees.

1. A Few Words about Shop Stewards

Before going into the legal details of "management rights," something important must be kept in mind. No matter what has been bargained for, it will not be worth much if it is not enforced on the shop floor. The shop steward or grievance person is therefore the most important day-to-day defense against management. Put another way, the steward is the daily defender of workers' rights.

Here are some of the things for workers and stewards to keep in mind:

—Workers are guaranteed the right to have shop stewards by Section 7 of the NLRA.

—How stewards are selected is up to the union. The number of shop stewards per worker or department or factory is determined by collective bargaining. Make sure you demand an adequate number.

—Stewards must be given "reasonable" means to do their job—time to see workers, write grievances, etc. However, it is best not to rely upon the law alone here because "reasonable" is subject to various interpretations. Be sure that the steward's rights are spelled out in detail in your contract. Otherwise, any time management tries to restrict the steward's activities (by not allowing a union bulletin board, refusing to provide a steward with space for his/her work, by not allowing the steward to move around the plant to check into the grievances on company time, by refusing to let the steward enter the plant on union business during the steward's nonworking time, etc.), the union will have to file an unfair labor practice charge with the NLRB. This takes a lot of time, and the NLRB might rule against you. You will have to show in each case that the company has violated Section 7 rights by its actions. You probably will have a good chance to win, but why take the trouble? Get the steward's rights in your contract. Then you can file a grievance if the employer disregards the contract.

—The NLRB says that a worker has a right to have a steward present at any meeting with management *if* the worker has good reason to believe that he/she is going to be disciplined.[25] In other cases no such right exists, and the Reagan NLRB has ruled that an employer's discipline of a worker denied a union representative will stand if the employer had just cause for the discipline.[26] So, again spell out the right of workers to have stewards present upon request at *all* meetings.

2. The NLRA and Management Rights

Section 8(d) of the NLRA says that employers must bargain with a union over wages, hours, terms and conditions of employment. Some unions have taken this to mean that everything which conceivably affects workers is negotiable. Such a view is anathema to employers, whose profits depend upon their ability to control workers. Especially critical to this control is the ability to unilaterally determine the size of the work force, what products are produced, the price of the product, the location of the plant, how the work is done, and so on. Whenever unions have tried to bargain over items like these, employers have seen red. The auto companies have refused to bargain over the speed of the assembly line and have rejected out of a hand a UAW proposal to raise wages but not the price of cars.

Most unions in the United States have granted employers the sole rights to make many important production and employment decisions. Managements have demanded, and unions have accepted, so-called "management rights" clauses in contracts which guarantee to employers many arbitrary rights. A good example of a management rights clause is as follows:

> The management of the plant and the direction of the working force, including the right to hire; discharge for just cause, suspend, discipline, promote, transfer; to decide the machine and tool equipment, the products, methods, schedules of production, processes of manufacturing and assembling together with all designs and engineering, and the control of raw materials, semi-manufactured and finished parts which may be incorporated into the product, shall be vested exclusively in the Company.

In other words, the company can change any of the things mentioned in the clause without discussing it with the union or violating the agreement.

Suppose that a union did try to bargain over something like the method of production (technology) used by a company or the location of its plant or the quality of the product made. In addition to opposition from the company, the union would also face a legal hassle. The Supreme Court said in 1958 in *NLRB v. Borg-Warner Corp.*[27] that certain matters, usually like those included in the management rights clause quoted above, are nonmandatory bargaining subjects. An employer can bargain over a nonmandatory subject but does not have to and cannot be charged with bargaining in bad faith for refusing. And if the union tries to force the employer to bargain by threatening to strike, it will violate the NLRA, and if it does strike, its strike can be enjoined. So, if your union wants management to agree that all first-line supervisors must be elected by the workers, you could not force the company to negotiate this and you could not legally strike to win it. The Supreme Court did in *Borg-Warner* what the NLRA *does not specifically do*—protect "management rights."

3. Plant Closings

Despite *Borg-Warner*, workers do have some legal protection from "management rights." Often when an employer exercises a "management right," workers suffer a deterioration in their "terms and conditions of employment." A simple (and a very important example today) would be if the employer decides to permanently close a plant. Shutdowns have a devastating effect upon workers not only economically but physically and emotionally as well. The NLRB and the courts have ruled that while, generally speaking, a union cannot compel an employer to bargain over its right to shut its plant (a mandatory subject), it can make the employer bargain over the effects of the shutdown.[28] A similar argument has been applied to the introduction of new technology, which often is like a partial shutdown from the workers' viewpoint. However, both the NLRB and the courts have given unions some right to bargain over the decision to subcontract work, especially when there is a significant effect upon the employment of bargaining unit workers (see Q62). Recent Supreme Court and NLRB decisions have drawn a clear distinction between subcontracting and a closing of part of an employer's business. In one case, a company which provided cleaning, housekeeping, and other such maintenance services to other companies ended a contract with one of its customers some days after a union had won a certification election there. The union filed unfair labor practice charges arguing that the company had to bargain its decision to terminate this contract. The Supreme Court ruled for the company, accepting the employer's claim that the decision was based upon purely economic considerations.[29] In a subsequent case, the NLRB ruled that a company could move an operation from one plant to another without bargaining with the union if the reason for doing so was part of an economically motivated reorganization.[30] In reality, these decisions can allow a business to win the benefits of subcontracting without having to bargain with the union about its decision.

Let us look at plant closings more carefully. A recent study stated that "between 1969 and 1976 at least 15 million jobs appear to have been destroyed in the U.S. as a direct result of plant shut-downs."[31] Since everything workers have won goes down the drain when a plant closes and since hundreds of plants are closing each year, it is important to know what workers can do when faced with a shut-down. (Q63 tells what to look for if you suspect a plant is going to be closed.) At present, you cannot legally prevent the closing unless the employer has agreed in the contract not to close the plant. However, a union can make it more costly for a firm to shut down, especially if it is simply going to move to a new location. It can do this by getting good contract language in the following areas:

1) *Advance Notice.* The employer has to give advance notice to the union and to the employees of any decision to shut down, completely or partially, move operations, seal the plant, contract out any work, or introduce any new technology. The advance notice should be as long as possible, but probably not less than six months.

2) *Transfer Rights.* Workers have the right to transfer to other plants of the employer with no loss of wages, benefits, or security. At least part of the moving expenses must be paid by the employer. The employer must train its workers for any new jobs available.

3) *Income Maintenance.* Here severance pay and supplemental unemployment benefits will help to maintain the income of workers who lose their jobs as a result of the employer's actions. Early retirement language should also be included.

It is best to have these things in the contract before the employer decides to act. Then you have strong legal grounds to make it obey the contract. But if you do not have such provisions in your contract, as soon as you learn of the employer's intentions, you can demand that the employer negotiate them with the union. The problem is that once management has decided to shut down, your bargaining strength may be so weakened that your union will not be able to win many concessions. Unless a union can mobilize broad community support, it will not prevent a company from closing by going on strike.

A recent and ominous development in plant closing situations involves companies which declare bankruptcy. When a business declares bankruptcy, it must go before a bankruptcy judge who has very broad powers to reorganize the business and to change its liabilities. The judge can actually reduce the company's obligations. Some bankruptcy judges consider collective bargaining agreements as mere obligations and have simply declared them null and void, meaning that the bankrupt employer no longer has to obey the contract's terms. Recently, a judge dismissed an agreement between Braniff Airlines and the International Association of Machinists. He did this because workers to be called back under a reorganization plan refused to give up their contractual seniority rights.[32] And this judge's decision was in effect ratified by the Supreme Court in early 1984 in *NLRB v. Bildisco and Bildisco.*[33] Here the high court ruled that a company can temporarily terminate or change a collective bargaining agreement when it files for bankruptcy but *before* the bankruptcy judge makes a decision. Once again the Supreme Court, now dominated by judges aggressively hostile to organized labor, gave employers a powerful weapon with which to weaken the labor movement. This was especially so since under current bankruptcy laws a company can file for bankruptcy based not upon its current losses but upon probable future losses! Fortunately, Congress, under strong and (for a change) successful pressure from organized labor, overturned *Bildisco* by modifying the bankruptcy laws. While a bankruptcy judge can abrogate a collective bargaining agreement, an employer cannot unilaterally do so. [34]

4. Successorship

Another problem which confronts unions in shutdown situations is successorship. What happens if another company buys the one where you work? Does your old contract bind the new employer? It does if you have a strong successorship clause in your contract. Here is a good one from an International Woodworkers of America contract:

> This agreement shall be binding upon the parties hereto, their successors, administrators, executors and assignees. In the event the entire operation is sold, leased, transferred, taken over by the sale, transfer of interest, lease, assignment, receivership or bankruptcy proceedings, such operations shall be subject to the terms and conditions of this Agreement for life thereof. The Company shall give notice of the existence of this Agreement to any purchaser, transferee, lessee, assignee, etc., of the operation covered by this Agreement or any part thereof. Such notice shall be in writing with a copy to the Union no later than the effective date of sale.

If the company violates this clause, by selling out to a company which does not agree to honor the old contract, the union can get a court injunction to stop the sale or it can sue the old employer for losses suffered as a result of the sale.

Where there is no successorship clause, unionized workers still have some protection, although it has been watered down by the Supreme Court.[35] If your plant is taken over through a simple sale of its assets (rather than through a merger), the new employer does not have to honor the old contract unless it agrees to or unless it lives up to the old agreement for some time after the purchase. If the new employer does neither, then about all the union can do is force the new employer to the bargaining table *if* the new employer retains a "significant portion" of the old workforce. Naturally buyers will say that they are going to hire new workers and will do so to avoid a duty to bargain. But in this case it might be possible to show that the buyer did this just to avoid bargaining, in which case it would be committing an unfair labor practice. If you can show that the buyer planned to use most of the old work force, then you can compel it to negotiate any changes in wages, hours, or grievances before the purchase. Also, if the buyer was aware of any unsettled grievances before the purchase, then the buyer has the same liability as the old employer would have to abide by any arbitration decisions. Finally, if the buyer hires a majority of the original workers, the buyer has to agree to arbitrate certain grievances which arose under the old contract, for example, the survival of seniority rights.

Two other elements of successorship law should be mentioned. First, as is true for shutdowns, the decision to sell is not negotiable but the effects of the sale are.[36] The employer must notify the union of its intention to sell and must bargain about the effects of the sale. However, since bargaining does not compel the employer to agree to anything, this isn't much of a right. Second, if the union can show that the successor employer is really the seller in a disguised or "alter ego" form, then the successor is bound by the seller's collective bargaining contract. The key here is to be able to show that ownership and control have remained in the same hands.[37]

All in all, organized workers usually come up losers in shutdowns and sales of their plants, and unorganized workers always do. New laws are badly needed, and workers hurt by plant closings, runaway shops, and takeovers are beginning to organize to get them. Most of the current proposals are patterned after Western European laws which sharply restrict the ability of a company to relocate, and which protect workers who lose their jobs because of relocations and shutdowns to a much greater extent than U.S. laws. Employers in Sweden, West Germany, and Great Britain, among others, must give long advance notice before closing (and *any layoffs* as well) and must negotiate the layoff or closing decision. National labor market boards must be notified, and these are empowered to initiate programs to minimize the effects of the employer's actions. In addition, workers' incomes are guaranteed more effectively than in the U.S. by better unemployment compensation and national health insurance.

In 1979, the National Employment Priorities Act was introduced to the U.S. Congress but not enacted. If something like it were to pass, firms would have to give advance notice of intent to close of up to two years to employees, unions, and a National Employment Priorities Administration. Employers would have to provide detailed justification for their decisions and guarantee a high fraction of both workers' incomes and community tax liabilities for at least one year. Ways would have to be explored to keep the business open, including the development of new product lines and government loans. A special penalty would be assessed upon a company planning to move overseas. Something missing from the NEPA but absolutely essential for workers is a guarantee that the community and/or the workers will have a chance to buy the plant with the help of government loans and subsidies.

C. Health and Safety

Most workers know that work can be hazardous to health. Every year literally thousands of employees die, are maimed and crippled, and contract diseases at their workplaces. Perhaps 100,000 people are killed every year by job-related diseases alone. A government study estimates that twenty percent of all cancer is caused by occupational exposure to cancer-causing substances. What's more, injury, death, and disease are not limited to coal mines and steel and auto plants. Postal work, for instance, is becoming increasingly dangerous; in 1979 a postal employee was killed when he got caught in a mail-sorting machine. Clerical workers suffer a host of ailments from blurred vision to numbed arms and shoulders. Health and safety problems are compounded by the inability of our economic systems to provide full employment. High unemployment itself causes poor health in the working class by increasing the incidence of high blood pressure, heart disease, and even murder and suicide.[38] It also allows employers to speed up work and cut costs in every possible way, making workplaces more unsafe and unhealthy.

If the labor law is weak with respect to discrimination and management rights, then with respect to health and safety it is pitifully feeble. One reason for this is that it is difficult for workers to organize around health and safety issues. Workers seldom know the health hazards of their work; harmful effects may not show up for many years. Since almost all occupational health and safety "professionals" work for industry, the working class has few knowledgeable allies to help it win healthier and safer workplaces. Finally, some workers have bought management's propaganda that most accidents are the result of employee carelessness and that it is not economically feasible to make work safe and less unhealthy. There is a lot of fear among workers that health and safety programs can come only at the expense of their jobs. UMW officials and many miners in Pennsylvania, for example, believe that overly strict environmental standards are one of the reasons why they are now unemployed. Needless to say, big business does everything it can to promote such thinking.

Actually, U.S. corporations spend very little money on health and safety by comparison with other advanced capitalist countries. The U.S. steel industry, which constantly complains about having to shell out large sums of money for anti-pollution equipment, actually spent only twelve percent of its capital investment in the 1970s on pollution control. The Japanese, who make steel much cheaper than we do, spent sixteen percent on similar controls.[39] Industries always overstate the cost of improving health and safety conditions and always ignore the benefits (longer lives for workers!). Consider this quote from a Ralph Nader study:

> In the early 1970s, for example, chemical manufacturers announced that a proposed federal standard on vinyl chloride, a proven cause of cancer, could cost 2 million jobs and $65 to $90 billion. "The standard is simply beyond the compliance capability of the industry," their trade association declared. The standard was adopted and industry has flourished—*without any job losses and at a cost that is one twentieth of the original industry estimate.*[40]

It might surprise you to know that many studies show that health and safety actually create jobs. "The Council on Wage and Price Stability [a government agency] did an inflationary impact study on the coke-oven controls and found that instead of causing a loss of jobs, the new regulations would result in 5,000 new jobs for technicians and maintenance workers to prevent leaks from the oven doors."[41]

Despite the obstacles which workers face in the struggle for safe and healthy employment, they have won a few victories.[42] Unionized workers usually have some kind of employer-financed health insurance which gives some limited protection against illness and accident. Some contracts provide for specific safety measures—prohibition of use of certain pesticides (United Farm Workers), mandatory use of safety equipment, periodic medical examinations, access to information on sickness and death rates and the right to the names of all chemicals used by the company (Oil, Chemical and Atomic Workers), paid union safety representatives (United Auto Workers), back pay for disabled workers (United Rubber Workers), and safety committees. A few union contracts specify that workers can refuse to work in unsafe conditions without penalty, although it is often not clear exactly what this means, especially if there is a no-strike clause in the contract.

Actually the National Labor Relations Act seems to give all covered workers the right to refuse to do unsafe work. Section 502 states "...Nor shall the quitting of labor by an employee or employees in good faith because of abnormally dangerous conditions for work at the place of employment of such employee or employees be deemed a strike under this act." However, in *Gateway Coal Co. v. United Mine Workers* (1974),[43] the Supreme Court gutted this provision by ruling that, where there is a no-strike or a binding arbitration grievance clause in a contract, workers cannot stop working unless they "present ascertainable, objective evidence supporting (their) conclusion that an abnormally dangerous condition for work exists." Needless to say, it is not usually possible to get such evidence. The Court's requirements for workers' use of Section 502 almost totally inhibit workers from using it, because unless they have " objective evidence" they can be disciplined by the company and any strike over safety can be enjoined. Suppose that miners suspect gas in their mine and refuse to work. The company disciplines them for an illegal strike. Then the gas dissipates. How could the workers prove that it was really there when they walked out?

1. Workers' Compensation Laws

Besides contract and NLRA "protection," most workers, after they are injured, can try to collect compensation under state workers' compensation laws. These laws were passed during the first decades of this century to give income to disabled workers without placing much of a cost or legal burden upon businesses. By 1910, several states had passed "employers' liability laws" which made it easier for workers to win suits against employers for occupational injuries and diseases. To counter this trend, corporations, through their lobbying and intellectual front groups, fought for and won state workers' compensation laws. These laws established payment scales for various types of injuries. Payments differ from state to state, but on average replace less than ten percent of the income lost by injured workers. Each state system is financed by premiums paid by employers to insurance companies. The insurance companies are, with five exceptions, huge private conglomerate corporations which pay out a mere 53 percent of the premiums they collect. Insurance companies have almost complete control over the workers' compensation system, from rate-fixing to benefit levels. This is very bad for workers because their health and safety are not the primary concern of the companies.

The workers' compensation system is totally inadequate, as is every aspect of state health and safety legislation. Benefits are ridiculously low and notoriously hard to collect; workers in most states must go to company doctors who, if the case is contested, will testify for the company; it is extremely difficult to collect for occupationally-caused diseases; and the laws do nothing to prevent injuries and diseases because it is cheaper for companies to pay the claims than to provide healthful, safe workplaces. Most states also have factory inspection laws, but these have never even been minimally enforced. However, if workers choose not to use the compensation/safety laws and try to take their employers to court, then the outcome will surely be worse. The burden of proof will be solely on the worker who must show that the employer was definitely at fault. This is nearly impossible in most occupational disease cases, and every worker knows how easy it is for the boss to argue that an accident was caused by worker "carelessness."

2. The Occupational Safety and Health Act

The years of corporate neglect of health and safety have, when conditions were right, prompted workers to rebel, sometimes forcing the companies and the government to respond with pro-worker actions. The most spectacular rebellion occurred in the late 1960s in the eastern coal fields. Tired of dying, being crippled, and especially getting black lung disease (which was not compensable under workers' compensation laws), miners, building upon years of organizing by Black Lung Associations, conducted a massive wildcat strike in February 1969. They struck, in opposition to their union's corrupt leaders, to get black lung compensation bills passed. As the direct result of their organization, strike, and marches, Congress enacted the Coal Mine Health and Safety Act of 1969 and the Black Lung Benefits Act of 1972. The first Act allowed miners or their widows to collect black lung benefits and "created a federal inspection system to enforce safety and coal dust standards." The second law presumed that any miner who has worked fifteen years in the mine has black lung and is automatically eligible for benefits.

Miners proved that organized militancy pays. Consider this amazing statement from Daniel M. Berman's fine book, *Death on the Job*:

> The annual payments [to miners as black lung compensation under the two laws] of over a billion dollars a year are 20 times the total paid out for occupational diseases for all other workers. In other words, 95% of occupational disease benefits in the U.S. are paid to coal miners and their families. For the first time in recent years the private sector lost control of workers' compensation, and company physicians have lost the right to determine what is a compensable disease. Federal expenditures for research on black lung disease jumped from $100,000 in 1963 to $7 million nine years later.[44]

Riding the wave of the miners' successes, trade unionists and their progressive allies won a new national health and safety law in December 1970, the Occupational Safety and Health Act (OSHA). In it workers were given the right to workplaces "free from recognized hazards that are causing or are likely to cause death or serious harm to employees." Some of OSHA's main provisions are the following:

1) It establishes an Occupational Health and Safety Administration (also OSHA) which sets safety and health standards for industry. OSHA can inspect workplaces and suggest remedies for violations.

2) Workers can ask OSHA inspectors to inspect their plants, and they can do this anonymously. Workers also have the right to go along with OSHA inspectors on their health and safety plant tours.

3) OSHA fines and orders can be appealed by employers, first to the Occupational Safety and Health Review Commission, a three-member board appointed by the President, and then to the federal courts.

4) In cases of "imminent danger," the Secretary of Labor can seek a federal court injunction to shut down a workplace.

While OSHA is a step in the right direction, it has not yet lived up to its promises. It has not always been enforced, and when it has been, penalties have been minimal. Between 1971 and 1975, fines averaged about $25 per violation, and only a small fraction of larger workplaces have been inspected. Employers delay enforcement by endlessly appealing OSHA penalties. The Supreme Court has further weakened the law by striking down Section 8(a) which allowed for OSHA inspections without a search warrant.[45] Now an inspector must have a court-issued search warrant, but the Court did say that a warrant could be given without the employer being present. In response to this decision the courts have begun, in some cases, to refuse to issue search warrants, sometimes after workers have been killed.

Under the Reagan administration, workers have gotten weaker OSHA enforcement. An important OSHA ruling giving workers the right to see their company medical records has been abandoned by the new OSHA administrators. Reagan's OSHA people believe that safety and health regulations must be justified on a "cost-benefit" basis. That is, the cost to the company or industry must be less than the benefits of the regulation before it is justifiable. This means basically that if regulation saves only a "few" lives and the cost is high, then the regulation must not be put into effect. Needless to say, business and its Reagan allies place very low value on the benefits of saved lives and better health! So far, the Supreme Court has refused to endorse this "cost-benefit" approach,[46] but, given the justices on the Court, there is no reason to believe that it will continue to do so. No doubt, none of the Justices has ever worked in a steel mill or a coal mine, nor has ever thought that the value of a miner's life snuffed out by an unsafe mine is incalculable to him/her and his/her family.

Reagan and company have targeted OSHA for destruction. A former construction boss, Thorne Auchter, was appointed to head OSHA despite the fact that his own company had been cited many times by OSHA for serious health and safety violations. Under Auchter, several OSHA films and booklets describing for workers how to use the laws and explaining the causes and consequences of brown lung were withdrawn on the grounds that they were too pro-worker. Auchter greatly reduced the number of workplace inspections. No longer can workers be assured that if they call OSHA, an inspector will come to their plant. Now an inspector will come only if the plant is in an industry with a safety record worse than the national average. Finally, standards already set for toxic chemicals have been lowered and new standards for other chemicals are being developed at a snail's pace if at all. In the past, for example, if a chemical was known to be toxic, a single standard was set for that chemical no matter where it was used. Now OSHA refuses to establish such "generic" standards and has substituted a case-by-case approach, in effect, possibly setting a separate standard for each use of the chemical. Naturally, this procedure will take forever to implement and will result in the injury, sickness, and death of thousands of workers.

One positive change, which was made by OSHA in 1985, is that a federal "Hazard Communication Standard" has been established which "requires manufacturers, importers, distributors, and some users of hazardous chemicals to participate in a complicated system of evaluating, classifying, and labeling such substances and making information about chemicals available for employees, employee representatives, and health professionals."[47]

As in civil rights matters, employers have become more sophisticated in getting around workplace health and safety laws. For example, rather than making a workplace safe for all workers, many employers have begun to "screen out" employees most susceptible to certain types of occupational hazards and illnesses. American Cyanamid Company refuses to let women of child-bearing potential work in their lead pigments department because future fetuses may be harmed by the mother's exposure to lead dust. Some women have actually had themselves sterilized to keep their jobs. Such corporate policies seemingly violate both OSHA and the Civil Rights Acts, but with Reagan's attacks on both laws, they are likely to become more prominent in the future.[48] Auchter's successors and several OSHA officials have been mired in scandal and corruption, ignored by most of the media, but deadly to workers.[49]

D. Minimum Wages and Maximum Hours

The Fair Labor Standards Act (FLSA) was passed in 1939 and has been amended many times since. The purposes of this act were to put a floor under wages (minimum wages), to force employers to pay overtime for hours in excess of some maximum, and to outlaw certain types of child labor. Today, most workers are covered by the law, and you can use it to sue your employer if you are not paid the minimum wage or the overtime premium (see Q64-65).

Probably the best-known part of the Fair Labor Standards Act is the minimum wage law (Section 6 of the FLSA). Congress has amended this section several times to raise the minimum wage. Since December 31, 1980, the minimum wage for covered workers has been $3.35 per hour. This certainly is an inadequate wage because if you work at this wage full time (around 2000 hours per year), you will still earn well below the official poverty level for a family of four. Congress could, and should, increase the minimum wage, but under the Reagan administration, it is unlikely that it will. In fact, there are proposals in Congress to lower the minimum wage for teenagers.

Almost all workers involved in any way in interstate commerce are covered by the minimum wage law. If your plant only buys and sells intrastate, you are still covered if your plant is part of a larger company which does deal in interstate commerce. However, there are some workers excluded completely from coverage and some others who are only partially covered. Employees of state and local governments were denied Fair Labor Standards Act protection by the Supreme Court in a 1974 decision,[50] but the Court reversed itself in 1985.[51] As a result of protests by state and local governments, Congress then amended the Act to allow such employees some special privileges in terms of overtime payments. In certain situations, state and local public employees may receive time off in place of overtime pay.

It should be noted that most states also have minimum wage laws for intrastate commerce. Be aware too that wages can be paid in other than money. They can include "board, lodging or other facilities."

Overtime provisions are in Section 7 of the Fair Labor Standards Act. Workers not covered by FLSA may be covered by state laws (the same is true for minimum wage). The overtime provisions and the rulings made on them are complex, and only a broad overview can be given here. An important thing to know is that the FLSA is not a maximum hour law except in the case of child labor. It only limits the number of hours at which your pay can be limited to your regular or "straight-time hourly rate." The rule is: you must be paid at a rate equal to one and one-half times your regular rate for all hours over forty *per week*. However, there are numerous complications and exceptions. Completely exempted from the overtime law are (among others) taxicab drivers, certain railroad and air carrier employees, many types of salespersons, domestic workers who live in the household where they work, employees of motion picture theaters, seamen, newspaper carriers, baby sitters, etc. Numerous groups are partially exempted from the law, but they are too complicated to go into. The best thing to do, if you are in doubt, is to assume that you are covered and make a complaint, at least to your employer, or an inquiry with an FLSA official, as outlined below, to find out for sure. For example, your employer might classify you as a "managerial employee" and not pay you overtime, even though you do not do managerial work. This is what Howard Johnson did. Workers were routinely classified as "assistant managers" and "manager trainees," but they performed no management functions. The Labor Department took the company to court in 1977 and forced it to pay back overtime pay.

Two other problems arise with overtime. What time counts as hours worked? What payments count as wages? Generally speaking, working time "includes all the time an employee must be on duty, or on the employer's premises or at any other prescribed place of work, or any additional time the employee is permitted to work." Time necessary to travel to and from work does not count unless provided for in a contract or by custom. Bonuses for extra production are counted as wages in calculating your regular wage, but items such as Christmas bonuses, profit sharing payments, and welfare plan contributions are not.

Section 12 of the Fair Labor Standards Act outlaws "oppressive" child labor. As with the minimum wage and overtime provisions, this part is also complex:

1) Children under fourteen are not allowed to work in *any* occupation or enterprise covered by the Act. There are some exceptions including actors and actresses, newspaper carriers, some farmworkers, etc. Generally, this work must be done outside of school hours.

2) Children between fourteen and sixteen cannot work in manufacturing or mining or as machine or motor vehicle operators. They also cannot work in construction, transportation, warehousing, communications, etc. There are, however, numerous exemptions and exceptions. A Department of Labor book titled *Child Labor Regulations* gives a list of permitted jobs for this group.

3) Children under eighteen cannot work at jobs declared to be "hazardous" by the Secretary of Labor. Some of these are mining, operating a sawmill or other machinery (except office machines), roofing, and excavation. To begin proceedings under the Child Labor provisions of the Act, you should contact the Wage and Hour Division of the Department of Labor, as explained below. Private suits are not possible for child labor violations.

Enforcement under the FLSA is nearly as complicated as the minimum wage and overtime provisions themselves. Basically, you have two choices if you think your employer has violated the law. You can sue your employer in federal or state court. Naturally you will have to hire an attorney to do this. In court you must prove that you are covered by the Act and that you have not been paid the minimum wage and/or overtime for hours which you have, in fact, worked. Your employer, if covered by the FLSA, must keep records of wages and hours and your attorney can get access to these records through subpoenas so that you can prove that you did the work. To sue in state court, you may also have to show that the employer owes you more than some minimum amount, which may vary from state to state. In federal courts there are no minimums, so for small amounts of money it may be wiser to sue in federal court.

Suits can be brought by individual employees or by groups of employees, but each member of the group must give written consent before the suit is actually brought. In court, you can sue your employer for back wages due *plus* costs (attorney's fees, etc.) plus what are called "liquidated damages." Liquidated damages are basically payments for losses which you suffer because your employer violated the law; these are in addition to the wages you actually lost. For example, had your employer paid you, you might have bought an interest-bearing asset (a government bond perhaps) or taken your kids to the dentist. So, the employer's failure to pay you cost not just your wages but also the interest you might have earned on the bond or the dental health of your children. Liquidated damages cannot be larger than the back wages you are suing to get; if you are suing for $1000 in back overtime pay, the damage cannot exceed $1000. Therefore, if you won, you could get $1000 (back overtime) plus $1000 damages plus costs. Ordinarily, however, the courts will not award damages unless it can be shown that the employer intentionally violated the law.

Your second choice is to go through the U.S. Department of Labor, which administers the Act. Within the Department of Labor, the Wage and Hour Division handles violations of the Act. The Administrator of the Wage and Hour Division is the person directly responsible in violation cases, although the Secretary of Labor is involved in the actual suits. If you have a complaint and you do not want to (or can't afford to) sue yourself, contact the Wage and Hour Division of the U.S. Department of Labor. There are regional offices around the country, so look in your phone book (or nearest large city phone book) under United States Government for Department of Labor (Wage and Hour Division). Call this office. You can make your complaint over the phone, or you can get a special complaint form to fill out. Once the Wage and Hour Division gets your complaint, it will investigate it and, if it deems it valid, will send an inspector to your workplace. If the inspector does find a violation, the inspector informs the employer. An informal agreement to pay the money due can then be made. If the employer refuses, the central Wage and Hour office can take the employer to court. Court proceedings can take several forms. The Secretary of Labor can sue the employer to recover exactly the same amounts which you could have tried to recover in a private suit. Curiously, the Secretary can sue without your permission. If this happens you lose your right to sue privately. The Secretary can avoid a full-scale court case by asking for an injunction in civil court to stop violations of the law now and in the future. As a part of the injunction suit, the Secretary can ask the court to order payment of any back minimum wages and/or overtime due. Unfortunately, an injunction suit can also be filed without your consent, and such a suit not only bars you from filing a private suit but makes it impossible for you to collect liquidated damages and costs.

One final point should be remembered. You must begin proceedings against your employer within two years of the alleged violation. Otherwise your suit or complaint will not be considered. The only exception to this is, if it can be shown that your employer "willfully" violated the law, then the statute of limitations is three years.

E. Pensions

Before World War II, pensions were reserved for managerial employees. Most people worked as long as they were able and then lived meagerly on what little they might have saved. This situation began to change during the Great Depression with the passage of Social Security legislation. Today over 90 percent of all workers receive at least a small pension from Social Security. However, Social Security has never provided adequate retirement income, so unions have, since World War II, bargained for private pension plans to insure their members a decent living during retirement. At first, employers refused to bargain on the subject of pensions, claiming that they were not "mandatory" bargaining items. But the NLRB in 1948 declared pension and other welfare plans to be mandatory subjects, opening the floodgates for pension bargaining.[52] Today, almost every collective agreement contains a pension plan.

Pension bargaining is complex, so let us define a few terms before discussing pension law:

1) *Funding.* This refers to the money (funds) out of which pensions are paid. A pension plan is "funded" if money is set aside in a fund to be used only for paying the pensions. A pension plan is "unfunded" if no such fund exists. Unfunded plans can be "pay as you go," in which case the employer pays pensions out of current revenue. Or, an unfunded plan can be one in which the employer pays premiums to an insurance company, and then the insurance company is liable to pay the pension.

2) *Vesting.* When a pension plan is "vested," the employee has a right to pension benefits even if he/she quits working for the employer whose plan covers him/her. For example, suppose you work for a company with a pension plan which provides for vesting after ten years. If you work for this company for at least ten years, you are eligible for some pension benefits when you retire regardless of whether or not you are working for this employer when you retire. An "unvested" plan is one in which workers lose their pension eligibility when they change employment.

3) *Portability.* If, when you change jobs, you can continue being covered by the same pension plan as before, you have a "portable" pension. A pension plan can be "vested" but not "portable."

As the workers who won pension programs during the late 1940s and early 1950s retired, pension horror stories started to surface. Pension funds did not have adequate funds to pay benefits. Some funds were mismanaged, and a few were depleted through corruption and theft. Workers discovered that no provisions had been made for pension payments in the event that their employer closed the plant or went out of business. Many plans had obscure rules, not known to the workers, stating that to collect a pension, a worker had to have so many years of continuous service. If there had been a break in service due to something not specifically approved by the plan, the employee could not collect a pension!

Pension abuses became so widespread by the 1970s that the labor movement decided that decisive action was necessary. Collective bargaining alone was not enough; federal legislation was needed. Congress responded in 1974 with passage of the Employee Retirement Income Security Act (ERISA). With this law, the most obvious forms of pension abuse were made illegal. The Act is administered jointly by the Department of Labor and the Internal Revenue Service. Workers who think that their rights under the ERISA have been violated can file suit against the managers of their pension plan (who may or may not also be their employer). In some cases, the Secretary of Labor may file suit. You (through your union) should contact a local Department of Labor or IRS office to get the details on filing suits.

The most important provisions of ERISA are the following:[53]

1) Employers and pension managers (called trustees) must file all of the details of pension plans, including financial statements, with the federal government. These details must also be made available to workers who participate in the plan.

2) Plan managers must manage pension funds prudently; that is they must use the "care, skill, prudence and diligence under the circumstances prevailing, that a prudent man acting in like capacity and familiar with such matters would use in the conduct of an enterprise of like character and like aims..."

3) Workers cannot usually be denied eligibility for a pension plan because of their age or length of service. However, for ERISA to apply, an employee must be twenty-five years old, have at least one year of service with the employer and not be within five years of normal retirement age.

4) All pension plans must be vested for all employees who have earned five years of work credit (1000 hours of work for pay in a year equals one year for vesting purposes).

5) Limitations are placed upon the loss of pension benefits for employees who, for reasons not their fault (sickness, leave of absence, etc.), have a break in their service with their employer.

6) All pension plans must be minimally funded. If the employer terminates a plan (by closing a plant or going out of business for example) and if there is not money available to pay the promised benefits, the employer can be forced by the government to make these funds available.

7) "Defined Benefit" pension plans, that is, those based upon years of service multiplied by some dollar amount per year of service, are guaranteed by the federal Pension Benefit Guarantee Corporation (PBGC). PBGC gets the money to guarantee pension benefits by assessing premiums upon pension plans and by having power to obtain $100 million from the federal treasury.

8) Workers can choose to make their pension benefits payable to their spouses or other survivors, but if they do, they may legally be required to take lower pension payments themselves.

Although ERISA is an advance over what existed before, it still leaves a lot to be desired. First, it does not cover public employees, many of whose pension plans are not in good shape. Second, it does not force all employers to have pension plans nor does it set minimum pension payments or compel plans to make cost-of-living adjustments. Third, the Act itself has encouraged employers to terminate existing pension plans because it does make them more expensive. The law should at least state that existing plans cannot arbitrarily be terminated. Today, more pension plans are being phased out than are being started. Finally, unions cannot legally force employers to bargain for increased pension benefits for workers already retired. The Supreme Court ruled that since retirees are not "employees," they are not covered by the NLRA.[54] Therefore, a union cannot legally force (by picketing, striking, etc.) an employer to bargain for cost-of-living raises for pensioners.

The major overhaul of the federal income tax which Congress passed in 1986 included some major pension law reforms, the most important of which is automatic vesting after five instead of ten years of work as was previously the case.

Chapter 5 _____

QUESTIONS AND ANSWERS

A. How To Use This Chapter

This chapter consists of questions which you might have about the labor laws and answers which will hopefully help you to use the labor laws to your advantage. The questions and answers are organized by topic, following as closely as possible the materials discussed in the first four chapters. Included in the answers are references to other readings which provide more detailed answers to a question than I can give. Where possible I tell you how to get copies of these readings, but be advised that the addresses and prices quoted are accurate as of the publication date of this book and are subject to change. So do not be surprised if it takes you a while to track some of these references down. I have copies of most of them, so if you are in a bind, write to me and I will see if I can make you a copy (Michael Yates, Department of Economics, University of Pittsburgh at Johnstown, Johnstown, PA 15904).

B. Researching the Labor Law

Question 1: *How exactly do we go about researching the legal ins and outs of a labor law problem? How can we find out just what are our rights?*

First of all, if your problem is at all complex, you eventually are going to need to hire a lawyer. If you are fighting a grievance through your union then you can probably rely on the union's legal experts, but otherwise you will have to find your own lawyer. Labor lawyers are often hard to find, especially in small towns, and any lawyer is likely to be expensive. The best thing to do is to shop around, ask questions until you find a competent attorney. It is best to have support from your fellow workers if you want to take on your employer so that a large number of people can pay the legal fees. Also, in cases where you or a group of workers are seeking monetary damages, some lawyers will work on a "contingency fee" basis, charging you a percentage of the money you win. If you lose, you do not have to pay the lawyer. Check into this possibility. Depending on the type of problem you have, you could also try to get in touch with organizations which might give you help: the American Civil Liberties Union for civil liberties cases (look in the phone book for addresses and phone numbers); the National Lawyers Guild (phone book or National Lawyers Guild, National Labor Committee, 558 Capp St., San Francisco, CA 94110) for all types of cases; Association for Union Democracy YWCA Bldg., 30 Third Ave., Brooklyn, NY 11217, (718) 855-6650 for legal hassles with your union.

Whether or not you get a lawyer, you can do a lot of the legal leg work yourself. The more you know about your rights before you take action, the better off you will be. For some preliminary information about problems which involve the National Labor Relations Act, you can call the nearest regional office of the NLRB, probably located in the largest city near you. Ask for the "information office," tell them your problem and ask them what you can do about it. For civil rights problems, call the nearest Office of Equal Employment Opportunity. Inquires on wages and hours can be made at the local office of the Department of Labor. Look in your phone book for the Department of Labor under "state government" for state laws and under "federal government" for the federal law.

To further research a labor law problem, you will need to have access to copies of the labor laws themselves as well as summaries of relevant NLRB and court decisions. In his booklet *Labor Law for the Rank and Filer* (available for about $2 from Miles and Weir, Ltd., Singlejack Books, Box 1906, San Pedro, CA 90733), labor attorney Staughton Lynd recommends the following books which can be obtained from many libraries:

a) *Federal Labor Laws.* This is a collection of the texts of the Federal labor laws, available for about $15 from West Publishing Co., 50 West Kellogg Blvd., St. Paul MN 55102.

b) *The Developing Labor Law.* This book describes the interpretations of the provisions of the NLRA by the NLRB and the courts. You can use it to find basic information about many labor law topics and to get references to NLRB and court decisions. It is available from Bureau of National Affairs, 2550 M St. NW, Suite 699, Washington DC 20037, for about $35.

c) *Labor Relations Expediter*. This book is kept in loose leaf form and is regularly updated. It would be too costly to buy, but you can use a copy at any law library. There is probably a law library at the nearest courthouse or university. In the *Expediter*, labor law topics (boycotts, picketing, strikes, etc) are given "key numbers"; for example, "Bargaining Units" have 63 and 64 as key numbers. Then the Bureau of National Affairs publishes a *Cumulative Digest* of labor law cases indexed by key numbers. The most recent digests will have summaries of cases for each of the key numbers of topics which you can use to get up-to-date information on the problems which concern you.

d) *Labor Relations Reference Manual* (abbreviated LRRM). These too are in law libraries. The court cases summarized in the *Cumulative Digest* or mentioned in other reference works will refer you to the complete text of the decision in the LRRM which consists of many volumes. A reference, or citation as it is called, might read 84 LRRM 1319 (1973). You would go to volume 84 of the LRRM and turn to page 1319 for this 1973 decision.

Besides the reference books which Lynd mentions, you could get a book called *Labor Law Course* at the library or from Commerce Clearing House, Inc., 4025 W. Peterson Ave., Chicago IL 60646 for about $40. This book is part of an alternative reference system organized by Commerce Clearing House, but it is fairly self-explanatory. The *Labor Law Course* contains a brief history of labor laws, analyses of the labor laws, and summaries of important court decisions. It has a good description of the Fair Labor Standards Act, including information on the complex ins-and-outs of minimum wages and overtime, as well as a short section on public employee labor law.

If you are public employees, it may be more difficult for you to research the labor law because not so many books are easily available. Federal employees should get a copy of Title VII of the Civil Service Reform Act of 1978. I got a copy from a friend of mine who formerly worked for the National Federation of Federal Employees. This union has copies of the law, a good guide to it, and many other documents relating to federal labor law available for reasonable fees. You might write to them at 1016 16th St., N.W., Washington DC 20036, telling them who you are and what you need and asking them if these resources are available to non-members. Your Congressional representatives could also be asked for copies of legislation and/or government regulations.

State employees can ask their state legislators for copies of the state's labor relations law. A trip to your nearest courthouse library or the law library of a university might be helpful in tracking down relevant court and labor board decisions. Do not be afraid to ask for help. Current information on State labor laws can be found in issues of the magazine *Monthly Labor Review*, published by the U.S. Department of Labor and available in most libraries.

C. Injunctions

Question 2: *You say that the Norris-LaGuardia Act greatly restricted the use of injunctions in labor disputes. Yet courts seem to be issuing a lot of injunctions these days. Just when can injunctions be issued?*

First, Norris-LaGuardia only restricts injunctions by federal courts, that is, in labor disputes involving interstate commerce. If you work in intrastate commerce, your employer may be able to go into a state court to get an injunction which could not be granted by a federal court. Also, if there is an immediate threat of violence or damage to property or if there is violence by picketers or strikers, *any* employer could go into a state court seeking an injunction to prevent damages or stop them if they have already occurred. Violence and property damage by anyone (not just workers) violate state criminal statutes and can be enjoined by state courts. So, suppose that picketers damage the cars of scabs or beat some of them up. A state court, upon request by the employer, might issue an injunction enjoining such action and limiting the number of pickets.

Peaceful picketing can also be enjoined by state courts in states with right to work laws so long as only interstate commerce is involved. If a union, for example, peacefully pickets a nonunion construction site to pressure the employer to use only union labor, this is enjoinable in a right to work state. (See Q35 and Q36 for more on injunctions and peaceful picketing.)

The Taft-Hartley amendments to the NLRA once again give employers access to federal court injunctions. However, the NLRA does not, with one exception, allow employers to seek injunctions directly. Rather, they must go through the NLRB which actually goes into court to ask for the injunction. But even though this is the case, Taft-Hartley definitely weakened the Norris-LaGuardia Act. Here are some situations in which federal court injunctions can be issued in labor disputes:

a) The NLRB can, but does not have to, seek an injunction to stop an unfair labor practice by either an employer or a union after it has issued an unfair labor practice complaint. If you were fired or discriminated against because your employer committed an unfair labor practice, the NLRB could seek an injunction ordering your reinstatement pending a final determination of whether the unfair labor practice was committed.

b) If a union violates Sections 8(b)4(a), (b), (c) or 8(b)(7) or 8(e) of the NLRA, the NLRB *must* seek an injunction. Thus when unions use secondary boycotts (see Q37) or try to pressure employers to recognize them when an employer already has recognized a certified union, the NLRB must try to have the union's actions enjoined. Also, the NLRB must seek an injunction to stop a union from striking or picketing to enforce a "hot cargo" clause. Note that *there are no employer actions which the NLRB must seek to have enjoined*—another example of the anti-labor bias of the NLRA.

c) Private parties can seek injunctions in federal courts to stop breaches of collective bargaining agreements. If your union strikes in violation of a no-strike clause or over a matter which the contract says must be arbitrated, then such a strike can be enjoined at the request of an employer. Even strikes over safety can be enjoined in such cases.

d) The U.S. Attorney General can seek an injunction in any federal court to stop a strike that threatens a national emergency.

One final point: if you are a public worker, probably without the right to strike and maybe without even the right to bargain collectively, then your strikes, picketing, or other collective actions are much more susceptible to injunctions than those of private workers.

D. Organizing a Union

Question 3: *Are unions legal everywhere in the U.S. and in Puerto Rico?*

Yes; any worker, regardless of employer, is allowed to join a labor organization. However, there are several complicating factors which in effect nullify this right for some workers. First, private workers unprotected by the NLRA or similar state laws can be fired legally for joining a union, or may suffer other employer discrimination. Thus a supervisor can legally join a union, but does not enjoy the protection of the NLRA and cannot therefore accuse an employer of unfair labor practices. Second, all unprotected workers and public employees in some states can join unions but cannot legally compel their employers to bargain with them. Neither can such public employees strike to win collective bargaining rights. Third, many public employees have the right to collective bargaining but cannot strike to win their demands.

Question 4: *Do part-time employees have equal union rights with full-time employees?*

As far as the rights of employees under the NLRB and other labor laws are concerned, they are the same for part-time as for full-time employees. There is no reason, for example, why part-time workers cannot try to form their own unions or be in unions with full-time workers. However, employers may not want part-timers in a union with other workers because then it would be more difficult to use part-timers as replacements for full-time workers (during strikes, for example). Unfortunately, unions often do not try to organize part-timers and treat them like second class citizens when they do. This is a serious mistake because it hinders the development of worker solidarity without which it is difficult to struggle against employers effectively.

It is conceivable that part-time workers might be excluded from a bargaining unit which includes full-time workers, if, for example, they do significantly different work.

Question 5: *We are a group of workers who want to form a labor union. How do we go about doing this?*

You will probably want to be affiliated with a national union organization, so your first step will be to contact an appropriate union. Many unions have locals in nearly every city and region of the country. These locals will be listed under "Labor Organizations" in the yellow pages of the phone book. Choose a union carefully because some unions may not be right for you. Some are better at and more interested in organizing small groups of workers than others. Some unions have stronger organizations in some parts of the country than in others. A good starting point is to look for a union which represents workers similar to yourself. Try to contact some of its members and ask them what they think of their union. Some unions have become "catch-all" unions which will organize just about any group of workers, and one of these might be good for your group, especially if it is strong in your area or if you perform unskilled or semi-skilled work. Important "catch-all" unions are the International Brotherhood of Teamsters, the American Federation of State, County and Municipal Employees (only for public employees), Service Employees International Union, and even the United Steel Workers and the United Auto

Workers. When you contact a union, identify yourself and explain your situation. A good union will send an organizer who will meet with your group and explain the steps which must be taken to form a union. The organizer will answer your questions, explain what is legal and what is not during an organizing campaign, etc. Ask a lot of questions. You deserve to have the best union representation possible.

The labor laws which affect the formation of a union vary according to the workers involved. Private workers in interstate commerce, with the exceptions discussed in Chapter 3, are covered by NLRA laws and NLRB procedures. Private workers in intrastate commerce are covered by state laws as are all nonfederal public employees. Federal government workers come under Title VII of the Civil Service Reform Act of 1978. While many of the laws are similar with respect to union formation, not all state laws have good procedures. In some states, intrastate and public workers still do not have the right to a secret ballot election and cannot legally compel their employers to bargain with them. This means that you may eventually have to strike to get your union recognized, although for most public employees this is not legal.

The NLRA and those state laws patterned after it set forth the following general procedures for union formation:

a) You must show, usually by signing "union authorization cards," that there is sufficient interest in unionization for the NLRB to call for an election. Generally 30 percent of the people in the bargaining unit as you define it must sign authorization cards to satisfy the NLRB. The union organizer will supply these cards.

b) Once the authorization cards have been signed, you can ask your employer to voluntarily recognize the union. If the employer agrees and the NLRB is satisfied that the union represents the will of the majority of workers, then the next step is to begin collective bargaining. Chances are, though, that the employer will not voluntarily recognize the union. In that case you must petition the nearest NLRB regional office for a union certification election.

c) Your employer can agree to an election immediately upon notice from the NLRB, but if it does not, the NLRB office will next conduct an election hearing. First the presiding NLRB officer (called a hearing examiner) will check authorization cards to make sure that there is sufficient interest. Then the examiner will hear any challenges by the employer (or conceivably by a rival union) to the nature of the proposed bargaining unit. Generally speaking, a unit cannot contain supervisors, plant guards in a unit with other workers, or both nonprofessional and professional workers unless the professionals (nurses, teachers, engineers, etc.)

agree. Beyond these restrictions the wishes of the employees as to the nature of the bargaining unit are usually controlling. However, this is not always so. An employer could argue that your unit is too narrowly defined (for example, suppose it only included body shop workers in an auto repair garage) and the NLRB might agree, in which case your petition could be denied. Remember, the Supreme Court in 1980 denied teachers at Yeshiva University the right to an election on the grounds that they were all in fact managers at the school!

d) If your bargaining unit is approved, the NLRB will establish an election date (or dates) and designate polling places. On the day of the election, an NLRB officer will be at your workplace where he/she will set up a polling booth. The employer and the union have a right to assign poll watchers and to challenge any person whom they think should not be allowed to vote. Voting is done by secret ballot; the name of the union plus "no union" appear on the ballot. Depending upon the size of the unit and the number of polling places, the ballots may be counted right away or sealed and counted at a central location.

e) If the union wins and there are no challenges to the election, the NLRB will then certify the union and bargaining can then commence. The election may be challenged if one party accuses the other of unfair labor practices during the election. The NLRB or the courts can throw out an election and order a new one if they feel that unfair labor practices seriously affected the election's outcome.

f) It is possible, but rare, that the NLRB will certify a union without an election if the employer's conduct is such that a fair election is impossible. For example, some employers create a climate of fear during an election campaign by firing, transferring, and/or demoting union supporters; by interrogating workers about their union sympathies or to find out who the leaders are; by threatening to close down the plant or even to physically harm the employees; by offering pay raises or bribes; etc. Such gross violations of the law have been occurring more and more frequently; an infamous example is J.P. Stevens Company. In such cases, the NLRB has the power to order certification for the union even if it loses the election, because a fair election is no longer possible. Usually, before it will do this, the NLRB requires that a majority of the original workers in the proposed bargaining unit sign authorization cards. A Federal Court of Appeals ruled in a recent case that, in exceptional circumstances, the NLRB can order certification though the union had failed to get a card majority, but the Reagan Board has since held that it will not do this.[1]

E. Unfair Labor Practices

Question 6: *Is it legal for an employer to refuse to give a union a list of the names and addresses of employees during an organizing drive?*

Before the NLRB has ordered an election, this may be an unfair labor practice. The union would have to show that refusal to provide such a list violated the employees' rights under Section 7 of the NLRA. Most likely this would be true if the union, because of plant location or some similar factor, had very limited access to the workers. However, once an election date has been set (see Q3), the employer must send such a list to the NLRB regional office within seven days. The regional office then sends the list to the union.[2]

Question 7: *Can we talk about the union at work?*

Yes, but generally speaking, it must be during nonworking time. However, the National Lawyers Guild says, "If workers are allowed to talk while working, then they can also talk about organizing so long as it doesn't interrupt production or cause discipline problems."

Question 8: *What about soliciting authorization cards and distributing union literature?*

This is all right, but it must be done in nonwork areas of the plant and during nonworking time. Again, the National Lawyers Guild says, "If there is a bulletin board for workers to post personal notices, they can use it to post organizing notices also. If workers are allowed to distribute literature about other kinds of subjects in work areas, then they can also distribute organizing literature too, unless it causes litter or extra work or can be considered a safety hazard. The last three special circumstances can be used to prevent distribution even in nonwork areas, under extreme conditions."

Question 9: *Can our employer refuse to let us wear union buttons?*

No. This would be an unfair labor practice. An exception would be if this interfered with your job or was unsafe. Make sure the wording on the button or sign is "decent."[3]

Question 10: *Can our boss ask us whether we are in the union or not?*

Private interrogation by a boss is almost always an unfair labor practice. Be sure you write down and date what was said at any such meeting and try to get a witness who knew about the meeting. It is probably better not to refuse to go to a meeting because your boss could say he/she was not going to talk about unions.

If your boss asks you casually and not in private about the union, this may be an unfair labor practice. Of course, you do not have to answer the question. It would be an unfair labor practice to punish you for this.

Question 11: *Can our employer force us to attend a meeting about the union?*

Yes, on work time, of course.[4] And, the employer can say just about anything about the union as long as he/she does not threaten you or offer you some benefit to vote against the union. There are many things which can be threats or promises. Your best bet is to write down everything said. If you think a threat or a promise was made, discuss it with the union to see if it would be wise to file a charge of an unfair labor practice. Note also that showing a strongly anti-union film at such a meeting was held not to be an unfair labor practice. Here is an example of a speech which would probably not be an unfair labor practice. Notice how far employers can go in suggesting that unionization would ruin the company:

> I want to apologize for the fact I am going to have to read my remarks this afternoon. I would like nothing better than to talk with all of you informally and straight from the shoulder—with no prepared written material. Unfortunately, I am going to read my talk because under the circumstances that exist here...this week, I would not want to have my thoughts incorrectly referred to later on.
>
> Before getting into the principal subject of this meeting—the rerun election next Tuesday—even though it is to some extent a repetition of my remarks at the big meeting this afternoon—I would like to take a few minutes to review again the extremely competitive situation in which our company has found itself for the past twelve to eighteen months. I want to spend a little more time talking about competition because I cannot overemphasize the importance of this subject to all of us. The real basis for economic

security and growth for this plant...or any company for that matter, rests on how well we meet our competition head-on.

As I have said on numerous occasions, to folks in all our plants, it is a basic fact of economic life that no business can survive, let along prosper and grow, if it cannot meet and do better than its competitors. To the extent that (we)...can do better in providing quality cartons, at competitive prices, when our customers require them, then we will be doing better than our competition. These three things: quality, service, and competitive cost are what determine how well we can meet competition. And unless we can meet and do better than our competitors, the kind of security we all want just will not exist.

The kind of real economic security that we all want for ourselves and our families can only be secured by continuous full employment of our plants. And the only way to keep any plant operating is by being able to secure enough sales, at reasonable prices, to keep our equipment busy. (I know of no union or union contract that provides work for this plant or for any other plant.)

If a union imposes uncompetitive conditions on an employer it can make it almost impossible for the company to secure enough sales to provide full and regular employment. Some companies have even been forced out of business because they could not survive as a result of competitive disadvantage. There have been several recent cases in our own industry.

To repeat—no union or union contract can provide what this or any company needs to be successful—the ability to secure enough sales to keep its people and equipment busy. On the other hand, *irresponsible union leadership* or uncompetitive conditions can make it practically impossible for a company to do this. Competition then—or rather a company's ability to beat its competitors—is really the key to job security for all of us.[5]

Question 12: *Are union organizers who do not work for the company allowed on company property to organize employees?*

As a rule, no. However, if this means that they cannot gain access to the workers, then many courts have ruled that they must be given limited access to company property such as access roads, parking lots, company houses, etc.[6] For example, if a plant is surrounded by company-owned roads and it is not feasible to reach the employees as they leave those roads, then union organizers may be permitted to use a company parking lot. In California, the Agricultural Labor Relations Board gives United Farm Workers' organizers the right to leaflet and meet with workers (who usually live in isolated company houses) on company property during nonworking hours.

Question 13: *If two unions are trying to organize a group of workers, can the employer show favoritism toward one of them?*

Yes and no. Yes, if favoritism involves only expressing an opinion about which union the employer likes better. No, if the employer actually helps one of the unions—by, say, allowing one union's organizers access to the plant while denying it to the other.

Question 14: *How can a union (or group of workers) prove that employees were discriminated against because of union activity?*

Sometimes the discrimination is so obvious that not much proof is required, although you should always keep notes of exactly what happened, when, and to whom. On the other hand, some cases are not so clear cut. Suppose a union leader is fired during an organizing drive. But suppose also that at the time of the firing this worker was also violating a company work rule. Is this an unfair labor practice? It might be, but it would be up to the NLRB to decide. Commerce Clearing House's *Labor Law Course* (1980 edition, p. 1593) tells us that the NLRB uses the following guidelines in such cases:

1. The entire background, including anti-union activity;
2. Percentage of union members or leaders among the employees affected;
3. Admissions;
4. Statement of the discharging supervisor tending to show his state of mind;
5. Answers to complaints which do not deny the discrimination;
6. Failure to explain a discharge at a hearing;
7. Failure to call as witnesses management representatives having personal knowledge of the reason assigned;
8. Effect of discharge on unionization—whether or not the leading organizers and officials of the union have been eliminated;
9. Espionage directed toward identity of union members;
10. Extent to which the discharged employee engaged in union activity;
11. Relation in point of time of employer's action to employee's union affiliation or activity;
12. Disparate treatment of competing unions.

Question 15: *When the employer violates a contract, is this an unfair labor practice?*

No, not usually. A contract violation should be taken up in the grievance procedure which might mean that an arbitrator decides it. The NLRB does not get involved in contract violations unless these also violate the NLRA.

Question 16: *Give us an example of a contract violation which also is an unfair labor practice. What should we do in such a situation?*

Suppose that you are an aggressive shop steward. Your employer suspends you for being late to work. You think that you have been suspended not because you were late, but because you have been a thorn in the company's side. You could file a grievance under your contract to protest the suspension, or your could file an unfair labor practice charge, claiming that the company violated Sections 7 and 8(a)(3) of the NLRA. Any time your employer disciplines a worker because of union activity, the union may be able to claim both a contract violation and an unfair labor practice. Here is another example. After a strike, your employer refuses to reinstate you by claiming that you engaged in picket line misconduct. You say the refusal to reinstate is because of your strong support of the strike. You could protest your dismissal by filing a grievance or an unfair labor practice charge.

In cases like these you can file a grievance or an unfair labor practice charge *or both.* Grievances are usually settled faster. However, the NLRB will, in many circumstances, defer to or demand that the grievance procedure, including arbitration, be used first, and while the Board has the right to overrule the arbitrator's decision, lately it has been increasingly unwilling to do so.[7] This is not good policy, but it is again reflective of the Reagan Board's anti-labor ideology. Arbitrators are not always equipped to interpret labor law, and Congress never intended that they do so. Arbitrators are notoriously careful in wording their decisions because they must stay acceptable to both sides. Worst of all, NLRB decisions have some precedent value for all workers in its jurisdiction, while an arbitrator's decision only affects the employees involved in one particular case. Today, the Board routinely defers union discrimination charges to arbitrators, who really have no business interpreting the heart of the National Labor Relations Act. But, ironically, because the Reagan Board is so hostile to labor, unions often prefer deferral to a Board ruling which may possibly affect the whole country.

Question 17: *Can an employer legally threaten to close down or move a plant during a union organization campaign? Can the employer legally close a plant after a union has won an election?*

If the purpose or effect of the threat is to deny workers their Section 7 rights under the National Labor Relations Act, then the threat is an unfair labor practice. However, the "free speech" provision of the Taft-Hartley amendments gives employers a lot more freedom to say negative things about unions than did the Wagner Act. So the employer's statement must be clearly coercive and not merely an expression of opinion. If a supervisor made such a threat but was just expressing his/her opinion and could not carry the threat out, this might not be an unfair labor practice. Nonetheless, you should keep records of whatever your employer says (notes of speeches and conversations signed by witnesses, copies of letter and bulletin board notices, etc.) that you think is threatening. These will be useful if you decide to file unfair labor practice charges.

In the *Darlington* case[8] the Supreme Court ruled that an employer could close down a plant permanently for any reason including the victory of a union in a certification election. However, a "partial" plant closing (e.g. a closing of just one plant by a multi-plant company) could be an unfair labor practice if the purpose or result was to discourage unionization at any of these other plants.[9]

Question 18: *We suspect that our employer is using an outside consultant to bust our organizing drive. How can we tell for sure? Can we do anything about it?*

Union-busting consulting firms are spreading like wildfire. For high fees, these consultants will either teach a company how to try to keep a union out or they will do the dirty work for the company. In many cases the consultants simply tell the company to violate the labor laws and then show them the best ways to do it. In other cases they recommend that a company obey the letter of the law but violate its spirit. In either case the results are the same: workers are harassed, cajoled, and intimidated and may vote against the union. One of the most notorious of the union-busters is Modern Management Incorporated (better known as 2M), which worked with employers on 696 organizing campaigns between 1977 and 1979. Unions lost 90% of those elections! Although many large industrial corporations—Inland Steel, Dupont, IBM, etc.— use consultants, they are most commonly hired in the service sector of the economy. This is because the service sector is growing rapidly, is least organized, and relies most heavily upon low wage labor. Hospitals, banks, retailers, nonprofit agencies (charities, schools), etc., are the worst abusers of the consulting racket. If you work in the service sector and are trying to unionize, chances are your employer has hired a consultant. If you do not know this for sure, you will be better off to assume that it is true and act accordingly. Also, if you already have a union, you may still be up against a consultant because the union-busters also specialize in bad-faith bargaining and union decertification.

It is not that difficult to spot the consultant's handiwork. Usually there will be a sudden change in the management's relation to its workers. Here are some things to look for:

1. *A barrage of letters* from the supervisor (or some higher company official), all addressed personally to the employees, and all written in a certain format. The tone of the letters will be basically friendly. You will be told how well the company has gotten along with you in the past, how the employer's door is always open if you have complaints, how the company takes a personal interest in you and so forth. You will also be told, sometimes subtly and sometimes directly, that the union cannot and will not do much for you. The union will be called an outsider, interested mainly in collecting your dues. You may also be bombarded with "evidence" of widespread union corruption, complete with cartoons of fat, greedy union bosses and mean-looking thugs allegedly in control of the unions. Usually the letters distort the nature of collective bargaining, an effective technique when few of the workers have had any experience with it. You may be sent a card with all of the things the union has said it would fight for in negotiations. Then you are asked to go to the union organizers and try to get them to give you signed guarantees that you will win all of these things. Of course, nobody could guarantee you these things, but neither would the management. (Take a similar card to your boss and try to get him or her to sign it!)

2. *Close personal supervision* by your supervisors. Your immediate supervisors will be recruited to do the consultant's dirty work. They will watch people very closely to try to find out who the union supporters are. They may begin to privately meet with workers to find out the same thing and to recruit informers. (Private interrogations are illegal, so if you are forced to meet privately, make a note of the time, place and nature of the conversation for a possible future unfair labor practice charge) Supervisors will make derogatory comments about the union and may begin to harass and intimidate you. The whole idea is to create a climate of fear and distrust. In public service workplaces, employers will try to make you feel guilty for supporting a union by saying that unionization will mean poorer services for your

clients. Church-related service organizations (e.g. Catholic Charities) have gone so far as to imply that to be for unions is to be against the Church.

3. *New strict work rules* which may limit the ability of workers to communicate with one another. For example, union supporters might be transferred to places where they cannot talk to coworkers.

If you suspect that your employer is using a consultant, there are several things which you can do. First, since many consultants either tell their clients to break the law or to stop just short of breaking it, chances are your employer will commit unfair labor practices. Keep good records of all suspected violations so that you will have good evidence for unfair labor practice hearings. Second, if you can identify the consultant, you can charge it with unfair labor practices which occur. The NLRB (in April 1981) ruled that a consultant can be directly charged with unfair labor practices where it is given control by the employer over the use of supervisors in an anti-union campaign.[10]

Probably the best tactic to use against consultants is publicity. Union organizers must anticipate their tactics and tell workers exactly what to expect. There are a lot of effective things which can be said and done to counter the consultants. You can point out how much money your employer is spending on consultants, money which could be used to raise your wages and improve your working conditions. This is especially effective if your employer is a public service agency or a private company which receives public funds, because you can then publicize (through picketing, letters to the media and to your political representatives) that public monies are being used to deny you your legal rights. Five hospitals in Boston paid 2M more than $750,000 in Medicaid money to defeat union drives. As a result, the unions pressed for a public investigation which resulted in new rules which ban the use of such funds to pay labor consultants. You can also picket the consultant's offices and hold press conferences or give out press releases to make the public aware of what consultants do. You can use evidence gathered at Congressional hearings (ask your Congressperson for the records) to discredit consultants. AFL-CIO organizing director Alan Kistler testified before Congress that one consultant told a management seminar:

> It is my strong feeling that blacks tend to be more prone to unionization than whites. Now, you have the EEOC (Equal Employment Opportunity Commission) these days, and you have to follow the EEOC. But there is no reason for you to be heroes about this and interested in abstract justice or upraising the downtrodden. So don't be heroes about the

whole goddamn thing and fill up the work force with blacks. If you can keep them at a minimum you are better off.

Finally, here are some things you should read to get a clearer idea on consulting and what to do about it:

1. Kinsey Wilson and Steven Askin, "Secrets of a Union Buster," *The Nation*, June 13, 1981, pp. 725-728. This will be available in most libraries.

2. *Union Busting: How it Works, Where it's Leading, How to Fight it.* This is a pamphlet available for $2.50 from Working Woman and Man Bookstore, 613 W. 24th St., Minneapolis MN 55405.

3. "Union Busters," *Southern Exposure*, Vol. VIII, No. 2 (Summer 1980), pp 27-48. This issue of *Southern Exposure* magazine can be ordered for around $3.50 from P.O. Box 531, Durham NC 27702.

4. The national AFL-CIO has organized a clearing house for information on union busting. Write to Research Director, AFL-CIO, 815 16th ST. NW, Washington, DC 20006.

Question 19: *How is an unfair labor practice charge processed?*

First, you (usually through your union) file the charge with the nearest NLRB regional office. A form like that in Figure One must be completed. Then the regional office assigns the case to an NLRB field examiner or attorney. If the examiner cannot get a voluntary settlement but can convince the Regional Office Director that the charge has merit, the Regional Director files a formal complaint against the party charged with committing the unfair labor practice. This complaint is heard at a formal hearing by an Administrative Law Judge (ALJ). The ALJ makes a ruling. Either party may appeal the ALJ's decision to the NLRB itself. Any NLRB decision may be appealed to a Federal Court of Appeals. An Appeals Court's ruling may be appealed to the U.S. Supreme Court.

In the hearings, the General Counsel's Office of the NLRB is actually the prosecutor. If you are filing against your employer, your union can intervene in the hearing so that a union attorney can be present to question witnesses.

Figure 1:
An Unfair Labor Practice Complaint Form

FORM EXEMPT UNDER 44 U S C 3512

FORM NLRB-501 (8-63)	UNITED STATES OF AMERICA	DO NOT WRITE IN THIS SPACE	
	NATIONAL LABOR RELATIONS BOARD	Case	Date Filed
	CHARGE AGAINST EMPLOYER		

INSTRUCTIONS: File an original and 4 copies of this charge with NLRB Regional Director for the region in which the alleged unfair labor practice occurred or is occurring.

1. EMPLOYER AGAINST WHOM CHARGE IS BROUGHT

a. Name of Employer	b. Number of workers employed

c. Address (street, city, state, ZIP code)	d. Employer Representative	e. Telephone No.

f. Type of Establishment (factory, mine, wholesaler, etc.)	g. Identify principal product or service

h. The above-named employer has engaged in and is engaging in unfair labor practices within the meaning of section 8(a), subsections (1) and (list subsections) _____ of the National Labor Relations Act, and these unfair labor practices are unfair practices affecting commerce within the meaning of the Act.

2. Basis of the Charge (be specific as to facts, names, addresses, plants involved, dates, places, etc.)

By the above and other acts, the above-named employer has interfered with, restrained, and coerced employees in the exercise of the rights guaranteed in Section 7 of the Act

3. Full name of party filing charge (if labor organization, give full name, including local name and number)

4a. Address (street and number, city, state, and ZIP code)	4b. Telephone No.

5. Full name of national or international labor organization of which it is an affiliate or constituent unit (to be filled in when charge is filed by a labor organization)

6. DECLARATION

I declare that I have read the above charge and that the statements are true to the best of my knowledge and belief.

By _____ (signature of representative or person making charge)   (title if any)

Address _____

(Telephone No.)   (date)

WILLFUL FALSE STATEMENTS ON THIS CHARGE CAN BE PUNISHED BY FINE AND IMPRISONMENT (U. S. CODE, TITLE 18, SECTION 1001)

GPO : 1983 O - 413-947

F. Collective Bargaining

Question 20: *When we go to the bargaining table, can we have anyone we want to represent us? What about management?*

The law says "Employees shall have the right to...bargain collectively through representatives of their own choosing..." This means that you can choose any person you want to sit at the bargaining table. Your representatives do not have to be members of your local or of your union. For example, you could include your local's attorney on the bargaining team. The same rule holds for the employer. Some employers, for example, use professional negotiators to bargain for them. This is perfectly legal.

Question 21: *What are the legal duties of the union and the employer at the bargaining table?*

Both parties must bargain in "good faith." However, "good faith" is an ambiguous phrase. It does not mean that either side has to agree to anything. The employer never has to agree to any of your proposals, and you do not have to agree to any of the employer's proposals. If there is no agreement, the two parties have reached an "impasse" which can be settled in a number of ways (which will be discussed in a later question).

Even though bargaining in good faith does not mean agreeing to anything, the NLRB does have guidelines for good faith bargaining. To be bargaining in good faith, your employer must:

1) *Meet you at regular times.* Refusal to meet or continually cancelling meetings is a sign of "bad faith" bargaining.

2) *Provide the union with certain information when it is requested.* You have the right to ask for and receive payroll (wage and hour), job description, seniority, and similar data which are necessary for you to bargain effectively.

3) *Present counterproposals.* The employer cannot just give you a set of proposals and say "take it or leave it." Good faith bargaining means that if you give a proposal to the employer, the employer must respond to it. Again, though, this does not mean that the employer has to agree to it.

4) *Be willing to commit any agreements to writing.* Management cannot say, "We agree to your last wage proposal, but we do not want it in writing."

The NLRB applies these same criteria to the union as well because under Taft-Hartley, it is an unfair labor practice for the union to refuse to bargain in good faith.

Question 22: *Can an employer legally refuse to bargain over some things even though the union would like to?*

Yes; the company is only obliged to bargain in good faith over what the NLRB calls "mandatory" subjects. Basically, these are "wages, hours and terms and conditions of employment." Terms and conditions of employment cover many things, such as union shops, safety and health, rest periods, grievance procedures, etc. There are two types of subjects over which an employer can legally refuse to bargain. First, an employer cannot bargain (even if it wants to) over subjects forbidden by the law. Therefore, it cannot bargain over closed shops, union shops (and often agency shops) in right to work states, hot cargo clauses, obviously discriminatory clauses, etc. which are illegal under various labor laws. (Note: an employer does not have to bargain at all with a union of employees not covered by the relevant law, e.g. a union of supervisors.)

Second, an employer does not have to (but is allowed to) bargain over what the NLRB calls "permissive" subjects.[11] These subjects are somewhat vague, but they are primarily items which the NLRB thinks it should be the exclusive right of the management to control. You probably cannot use the law to force management to bargain over its right to buy another company, introduce a new technology, relocate or expand its plant, choose supervisors, sell the company, decide work schedules (number of shifts), set prices of its products, choose its suppliers, reorganize the management, and other similar things. Management is permitted to bargain over these items, but you cannot force it to. This means that you cannot legally strike or picket to try to compel the company to bargain over permissive subjects. The United Auto Workers once presented General Motors with a proposal by which the Company would agree to raise wages but not the prices of its cars. GM refused to negotiate this claiming that it had the sole right to set the price of cars. The NLRB agreed.

Sometimes a union can get around the problem of permissive subjects. Let's say that you do not want the company to move its plant. You cannot force it to say in the contract that it will not move. But you can force the company to negotiate the effects of a move. That is, you can force the company to negotiate severance pay for workers who lose jobs when the plant moves, relocation rights and moving allowances for workers who can move to the new location, protection of health insurance and pensions for displaced workers, etc. Anything you win here from the company makes it more expensive for the company to move and therefore less likely to do so.

Question 23: *What can we do if we believe that our employer is not bargaining in good faith?*

You have three choices. First, you can make your feelings known to the employer and threaten further action such as a strike or an unfair labor practice charge. Second, assuming that you are legally free to strike and picket, you can do so to force the employer to change its ways. You can strike and picket or you can just picket, either outside the plant or in any public place (you may have to get permission from public officials to do this). A public place would be a city street, sidewalk, park, or some similar place. Third, you can file an unfair labor practice charge against your employer with the NLRB (assuming you are covered). In the case of a refusal-to-bargain in good faith charge, however, it is important to remember one thing. When the NLRB determines that a company has not bargained in good faith, the penalty which it applies is just to tell the company to bargain in good faith. No money penalty is assessed.[12] Therefore, this really amounts to a slap on the wrist to the employer for breaking the law. It will not make a really hostile employer bargain seriously because it is a token penalty. If your employer continues to bargain in bad faith, you will have to file another unfair labor practice charge. Eventually, the NLRB might seek a court order to force the employer to bargain. If the company still does not bargain, it might be found guilty of contempt of court and then fined. This fine might make your employer bargain, but do not count on it. Usually the contempt fines are small, and some corporations would rather pay them than bargain. Besides it is very costly and time-consuming for the union to press the issue to the point of contempt fines. Finally, while you are doing this, your union might suffer serious losses of confidence from members. So, there is nothing wrong with filing an unfair labor practice charge when your employer refuses to bargain, but do not expect much in the way of results. Employer refusal-to-bargain has become epidemic over the past thirty years, especially during first contract negotiation. "...The rate at which unions obtained first contracts also declined steadily, from 86 percent of bargaining units certified between 1955 and 1960, to 78 percent of newly certified units in 1970, to 63 percent in 1980."[13] To remedy this, one author has suggested not just monetary penalties but binding arbitration to insure that a new union, often unable to mount an effective strike, will obtain a first contract.

Question 24: *Can an arbitration ruling be appealed to the courts?*

Usually, the answer is no. The Supreme Court has ruled that the decision of an arbitrator is binding and not appealable.[14] The only exceptions would be if the arbitrator's award itself violates the law or if there is a question about whether the dispute was arbitrable in the first place. The latter exception occurs rarely because the Court has also said that almost all disputes are arbitrable. You should note that an arbitration award does not necessarily prevent you from taking legal action to get what you want. For example, suppose you file a grievance charging your employer with racial discrimination in violation of a contract prohibiting such discrimination. The grievance goes to arbitration and you lose. You can still take your employer to court for violating the civil rights laws.

In certain circumstances a court may modify an arbitrator's award or tell the parties which parts of a dispute are arbitrable.[15] Suppose a company has two plants, each organized by a different union. Plant A shuts down, and the union demands to bargain over transfer rights of the laid-off workers at Plant A. This leads to a dispute which eventually goes to an arbitrator. The arbitrator awards the workers some right to transfer to Plant B. However, the employer argues that this award would force it to violate its contract with the union at B. In this case the court might overturn the arbitrator's ruling on the grounds that it does not promote the industrial peace which is one of the main goals of the NLRA. Or, if the company had refused to arbitrate the matter of transfers in the first place, a court might order the company to arbitrate, but might also limit the scope of the arbitrator's award so as to avoid a ruling which forces the company to violate another contract.

Question 25: *Can an employer petition the NLRB to have a union decertified?*

No, but there are two indirect ways in which an employer might be able to get rid of a union. First, suppose your local calls a strike in a bargaining dispute. Such a strike is called an "economic strike," and the strikers are called "economic strikers." Suppose your employer hires strikebreakers to replace you during the strike. The new workers could call for a decertification election (probably with some coaxing from the employer, though this is technically illegal). If the new election is scheduled less than twelve months from the beginning of the strike (which is still in progress), then both the strikers and their replacements can vote in the election. However, if the election occurs more than twelve months after the strike begins (again, the strike is still in progress), then only the replacements get to vote. So, an employer facing a weak union in an area where strikebreakers are available might actually instigate an economic strike, hire replacements who, after one year of the strike, call for a decertification election. This is precisely how the Joseph Coors Brewing Company got rid of its union in 1977 and 1978.

Second, an employer can legally refuse to bargain with the union which the employer believes no longer represents a majority of the workers (that is, most of the workers no longer want to be represented by the union). However, if there has not been a decertification election, it would probably be difficult for the employer to prove that the union no longer had a majority. One thing which an employer which has a "good faith" belief that the union has lost its majority support can do once a contract has expired or one year after union certification if no contract is in effect is to file an election petition. Such a petition is called an RM petition, and if the NLRB decides to conduct such an election, this could be a way for the employer to have the union, in effect, decertified.[16]

Question 26: *Our contract has expired. We have not agreed to extend it and have gone on strike. Do any of the provisions of the old contract still apply to us?*

Yes, but the Courts have not made many decision in this area, so exactly what parts of the old contract are still in effect is not clear. In a 1980 case, the NLRB said:

> Although an employer's contractual obligation ceases with the expiration of a contract, those terms and conditions established by the contract in governing the employer-employee relationship, as opposed to the employer-union relationship, survive the contract to present the employer with a continuing obligation to apply those terms and conditions, unless the employer gives timely notice of its intentions to modify a condition of employment and the union fails to timely request bargaining, or impasse is reached during negotiations of the proposed change.[17]

This means that the old wage scales, benefits, grievance procedure, seniority clause, etc. are still in force. Unsettled grievances can still be pushed to arbitration during a strike. Grievance claims can be made after the contract has expired if the employer action being grieved took place before the contract expired. Strikers may be eligible for holiday and vacation pay during a strike. Health benefits are still in effect. If the employer hires scabs, it must pay them according to the old contract. However, an employer can unilaterally change the terms of the old contract if it notifies the union of its intention to do so and the union fails to request bargaining on the proposed change. Presumably the NLRB will decide on a case-by-case basis how long the union has to request bargaining. If the union requests bargaining, the employer can still change the contract terms if the bargaining breaks down (reaches impasse). Of course, the union could claim that an impasse did not exist, and then it would be up to the NLRB to decide.

G. Strikes, Picketing, and Boycotts

Question 27: *What happens when negotiations break down?*

Any number of things can happen. Assuming that there are no legal prohibitions in effect (see Q28), the union can go on strike to force the employer to accept the union's demands. The company could lock the workers out to put pressure on the union in a situation where the union is not ready to strike. If *both* parties agree, a mediator can be called in. A mediator is a person skilled in getting labor and management back to the bargaining table, but the mediator has no power to dictate a settlement. The federal government and most states have public mediation services which can be used to help settle negotiating impasses. Your union will know how to contact these agencies. Or, you could use a private mediator (and split the costs). Mediators can be used to try to avoid a strike, or they can be called in after a strike has begun.

There are some situations in which the law says mediators must be used. This is true for nearly all public employees, including those few who can legally strike. In Pennsylvania, for example, public workers and employers would have to call in a state mediator before a strike could be called. In the private sector, a federal mediator must be used if the President declares that a strike has threatened a "national emergency" and gets an injunction to stop it for 80 days.

Another way to settle an impasse (bargaining breakdown) is to use an arbitrator. An arbitrator conducts hearings and then imposes a binding settlement on the parties. In most public employee situations, strikes are illegal and arbitrators must be used as a last resort where an impasse cannot be broken. Arbitration to settle bargaining breakdowns in private employment is rarely used, the main exception being the steel industry. In the "Experimental Negotiating Agreement" signed in 1974, the United Steel Workers gave up the right to strike when an impasse is reached in national bargaining. Instead an arbitrator was to be called in to make a binding decision. This agreement was eliminated from the 1983 contract.

Question 28: *Can a union legally strike at any time during negotiations for a contract?*

No. Workers covered by the National Labor Relations Act can strike any time after their contract has expired (or at any time if this is bargaining for a first contract) provided they have given their employer 60 days prior notice (90 days in the health care industry) of their intention to change the terms of their contract. If the contract has not yet expired, the union cannot legally strike if there is a "no strike" clause in the contract. If there is not a "no strike" clause in the contract, the union is free to strike but again the 60 day notice must be given if the union wants the terms of the contract changed.

Question 29: *Can union workers legally strike over a grievance dispute?*

Maybe. Suppose that a worker is fired for alleged misconduct. Your union files a grievance, but from past experience you know that it will be months before the grievance is settled and the worker reinstated (assuming the union wins the grievance). So, the union calls a strike to get the worker back. If there is a "no strike" clause in your contract, this strike is clearly illegal. Your employer could seek an injunction to stop the strike and could also sue the union for violating the contract. If there is not a "no strike" clause, the strike *may* be legal. But if your contract has arbitration as the final step of the grievance procedure and if it states that arbitration will be the only means of settling contract disputes, then your strike is still most likely illegal.[18] Thus, if your contract has a grievance procedure which ends in arbitration, any strike during the term of the contract may be illegal. One way in which this problem may be avoided is to have right to strike language in the contract. Or, if there is a "no strike" clause, make sure that it says that no strikes can be called until the grievance procedure has been exhausted.

Question 30: *Is an employer always free to hire strikebreakers during a strike?*

Yes; although transporting armed strikebreakers into a struck plant is illegal (an unfair labor practice) as is violence by strikebreakers. A federal law called the Byrnes Act says,

Whoever willfully transports in interstate or foreign commerce any person who is employed or is to be employed for the purpose of obstructing or interfering by force or threats with (1) peaceful picketing by employees during any labor controversy affecting wages, hours, or conditions of labor, or (2) the exercise by employees of any of the rights of self-organization or collective bargaining; or whoever is knowingly transported or travels in interstate or foreign commerce for any of the purposes enumerated in this section—shall be fined not more than $5,000 or imprisoned not more than two years, or both.

Question 31: *Do strikers have the right to get their jobs back after the strike if the employer has hired replacements?*

The reinstatement rights of strikers depend upon the nature of the strike. Economic strikers striking for better wages, hours, or terms and conditions of employment, do not have reinstatement rights if they have been permanently replaced. However, if there are vacancies, they must be given the vacancies. When new vacancies occur, the strikers must be given preference in filling them. An employer who refuses to reinstate economic strikers in the circumstances just described commits an unfair labor practice. A union can protect strikers by insisting that a part of the strike settlement is that any replaced workers *must* be reinstated.

If the strike occurs because the employer has committed unfair labor practices, then the strike is an unfair labor practice strike and the strikers are called unfair labor practice strikers. Unfair labor practice strikers must be reinstated after the strike, and the strikebreakers must be dismissed to make room for them.

An economic strike can become an unfair labor practice strike if the employer commits an unfair labor practice after the economic strike has begun. In this case, strikebreakers hired after the unfair labor practice have to be discharged and strikers reinstated when the strike is over.

Generally speaking, if workers engage in an illegal strike or engage in illegal activities during a legal strike (violence), they can be fired and have no reinstatement rights. (See Q34-36 for examples of illegal strikes and picketing.)

Question 32: *Does an employee who takes another job during a strike lose whatever reinstatement rights he/she might have?*

No, except that economic strikers need no longer be shown any reinstatement preference by an employer if they have obtained "equivalent" employment elsewhere. The NLRB and the courts may have to decide what "equivalent" employment is. If a carpenter replaced during a strike gets a permanent job as a carpenter at about equal wages, he/she would not have reinstatement rights. But if he/she got a job as a dishwasher, he/she would have reinstatements rights. However, other types of employment might not be so clear cut.

Question 33: *Can strikers collect unemployment compensation? Welfare?*

In only two states (New York and Rhode Island) can strikers collect unemployment compensation, after the strike has continued for some specified period of time. In some states strikers are eligible for some sort of general welfare assistance such as food stamps if they can otherwise qualify (the Reagan administration has tightened up regulations to eliminate many strikers). You should apply for public assistance and see what happens. There are some exceptions to the general rule that strikers do not qualify for unemployment compensation, so you might file a claim to see if you qualify.

Question 34: *Are "wildcat" strikes always illegal?*

The labor laws themselves do not say much about wildcat (usually walkouts, during the term of a contract, not called by the union) strikes. The NLRB has held that walkouts by unorganized workers to protest wages, hours, or terms and conditions of employment are, under certain circumstances, protected by the National Labor Relations Act. This means that if the employer disciplines the strikers, it may be committing an unfair labor practice. For this to be the case the workers have to be acting "in concert" (that is, together) and the wildcat must be an isolated event and not a part of a strategy aimed at forcing the employer to change wages, hours, and terms and conditions of employment.[19] The point here to remember is that you don't have to be already organized or even trying to form a union to be protected by Section 7 of the NLRA. However, it will be up to the NLRB to decide whether any particular walkout by unorganized workers is protected.

A different situation occurs when workers are trying to form a union and strike to force their employer to recognize their union. That is, when the union does not go through NLRB procedures to form the union. Such strikes are legal, but often risky. You cannot picket for more than 30 days without calling for a representation election. You could continue striking, but you could not picket. If you are economic strikers (wages, hours, etc.) you can be replaced by your employer and you have very limited reinstatement rights. If you are unfair labor practice strikers (your employer has committed an unfair labor practice), you are guaranteed reinstatement after the strike.

Finally, once you are unionized and have a contract, there is a much greater likelihood that wildcat strikes are illegal. First, if you have a "no strike" clause in your contract, a wildcat strike is definitely illegal because it violates or breaches the contract. The strikers are subject to injunction upon request of the employer, and the union is also subject to suit for money damages which may result from the wildcat. Wildcat strikes are usually not subject to arbitration either. It is legal to bargain for a contract clause in which both parties agree not to sue for alleged breaches of the contract. Such a clause protects wildcats from damage suits but not from injunctions. You could also make the right to sue subject to arbitration.

If you do not have a "no strike" clause, you still may not be free to strike if what you are striking about is subject to a grievance procedure which ends in binding arbitration. Court rulings have almost always held that arbitration is a better way to settle disputes over contract language than a strike. Therefore, a strike over, say, an alleged employer violation of the seniority provisions of the contract can still be enjoined even if there is not a "no strike" clause in your contract. This is true even for strikes over safety violations. You can refuse to work at an unsafe job; your coworkers cannot walk out to support you (see Q29 for details).

Question 35: *When is it legal to picket?*

Picketing law is complex,[20] and it is sometimes difficult to say for sure whether or not any particular picketing is legal. However, what follows are some rough guidelines. Remember that *primary* picketing is that in which you picket your employer, while *secondary* picketing is that in which you picket some other employer.

Violent picketing, no matter what kind, is always illegal, even in response to violence by the employer. Violent picketing violates the criminal laws of all of the states, and in addition it jeopardizes the reinstatement rights of strikers who engage in it (see Q31). State courts have also held that mass picketing, in which there are so many pickets that it is impossible for nonstriking workers or managers to enter a plant, is a form of violent picketing.

Peaceful picketing is, generally speaking, regulated by the statute and common laws of the states, which means that the law is different in each state. However, Congress has enacted laws which preempt or supersede state laws in some cases. The Taft-Hartley law outlaws nearly all types of secondary picketing. For example, if you picket an employer to which your employer makes deliveries, this would be an unfair labor practice because it is secondary picketing. Basically, any picketing used to support a secondary boycott (see Q37 for details and exceptions) is an unfair labor practice.

Taft-Hartley also regulates primary peaceful picketing in certain circumstances. If you are picketing to organize workers, you cannot picket for more than 30 days unless you call for a representation election. In such cases, the employer can call for an election after the 30 days. You cannot engage in organizational picketing (picketing to get an employer to recognize a union) within twelve months of a valid (certified) election. You cannot picket to force an employer to recognize a union when another union has already been certified. Informational picketing (to inform the public about your employer, e.g. its anti-union sentiments) is protected by Section 8(b)(7)(c) of the National Labor Relations Act which states, "...nothing in the subparagraph (c) shall be construed to prohibit any picketing or other publicity for the purpose of truthfully advising the public (including customers) that an employer does not employ members of, or have a contract with, a labor organization." Informational picketing is generally exempted form the exceptions to primary picketing, but in practice it is often hard to tell the difference between illegal primary picketing and informational picketing. If your union pickets an employer after another union has been certified, the NLRB probably will conclude that your purpose is to force the employer to recognize your union and not just to inform the public of something. Your picketing will therefore not be considered informational even if your picket signs meet the conditions of the proviso in 8(b)(7)(c) just quoted. If your informational picketing acts as a "signal" to other workers to stop dealing with a secondary employer, you are most likely engaging in an illegal secondary boycott. Suppose your union pickets an employer other than your own with signs which say that the employer is unfair to labor. Suppose also that this employer's workers stop working because of your picketing. Even though your picketing appears to be informational, you will still be engaged in illegal secondary boycotting because the effect of your picketing is to cause secondary workers to stop working.

What about peaceful primary picketing which does not violate Taft-Hartley nor enjoy its protection? Such picketing is regulated by state law, but the Supreme Court has declared some state laws to be unconstitutional and so has made it unlawful for states to declare some types of peaceful primary picketing illegal. For example, a 1940 Supreme Court decision made it unconstitutional for a state to outlaw all picketing, on the grounds that picketing is a form of free speech.[21] However, as future decisions have indicated, the Court did not mean to say that, because peaceful picketing was a form of free speech, it was always legal. Therefore, states can outlaw some forms of peaceful primary picketing. Here are some Supreme Court rulings.

1. *Carpenters and Joiners Union v. Ritter's Cafe* (1942)[22]: Mr. Ritter hired nonunion labor to perform construction work on his house. The union picketed his restaurant to protest this, and the employer asked for and got a state court injunction to stop the picketing. (Note that the Norris-LaGuardia Act did not apply because interstate commerce was not involved.) The Supreme Court upheld the injunction arguing that the union did not have a labor dispute with the restaurant.

2. *Giboney v. Empire Storage and Ice Co* (1949)[23]: The union got ice manufacturers and wholesalers to agree not to sell ice to nonunion peddlers. The Empire Company refused to go along and was picketed by the union. It sought a state court injunction, claiming that agreeing with the union would force it to violate a state anti-monopoly law. The injunction was granted and the Supreme Court upheld the state court. This decision means that picketing, the result of which may be a violation by an employer of a state law, can be made illegal, or a state court can use state "common law" to enjoin it.

3. *Building Service Employees' Union v. Gazzam* (1950)[24]: The union picketed a hotel to force the employer to recognize it as bargaining agent for the employees. It was known that most of the workers did not want to join the union. The Supreme Court upheld the injunction issued by the state court because it was state policy, as expressed in state laws, that workers should have free choice with respect to bargaining agents. (Note that this was an intrastate commerce case. Had it been in interstate commerce, the Taft-Hartley provision for organizational picketing would have applied.)

4. *Plumbers' Union v. Graham* (1953)[25]: The Supreme Court allowed a Virginia court to enjoin picketing of a nonunion shop because the state's right to work law made it unlawful to require membership in a union as a condition of employment.

5. *Teamsters' Union v. Vogt, Inc.* (1957)[26]: Here the Supreme Court allowed a Wisconsin Court to enjoin simple stranger picketing!

A question which you might ask about these cases is: what about the Norris-LaGuardia Act? Isn't picketing in support of a labor dispute not subject to injunction? Yes, in theory. In practice, Norris-LaGuardia is not what it used to be. First, it does not apply to picketing of companies in intrastate commerce. States can outlaw and state courts can enjoin all sorts of picketing when intrastate commerce is involved. Second, in cases where the employer is in interstate commerce, the picketing can still be outlawed or enjoined if the Supreme Court says that no labor dispute exists. This is the implication of most of the above decisions.

Everything said so far about picketing applies to picketing in public places (roads, streets, in front of plant gates, etc.). If you picket on private property you are trespassing, and you may be breaking the law. However, workers covered by the NLRA can sometimes picket (or pass out hand bills or talk to employees) on private property to organize an employer or to win a strike. The NLRB has to be convinced that the organizing effort or strike can have little or no chance to succeed unless the employees have access to the employer's private property. In such cases, the workers' Section 7 rights outweigh the employer's property rights. For example, a store in a shopping mall cannot be effectively picketed unless the pickets can enter the mall, which is private property. The Supreme Court ruled that it would deny workers their Section 7 rights to deny them the right to picket in the mall. Therefore, the picketing was legal. This is a tricky area, so you should probably talk with a good lawyer if there is any doubt. Of course, you may have to risk an injunction in any situation if your cause is just and the picketing is crucial to your victory.[27]

State legislatures and courts also have broad power to regulate picketing by, for example, limiting the number of pickets.

Question 36: *What is "common situs" picketing? Is it legal?*

Common situs picketing occurs when picketing takes place at a location occupied by more than one employer. For example, if electricians at a construction site picket the site, they are in effect picketing all of the employers who have contracted to work at the site. The NLRB has ruled that four conditions must exist for such picketing to be legal:[28]

    1) The picketing must be strictly limited to the times

when the site of the dispute is located on the secondary employer's premises.

2) The picketing must take place when the primary employer is engaged in its normal business at the site.

3) The picketing must be limited to places reasonably close to the site of the dispute.

4) The picketing must clearly say that the dispute is with the primary employer.

Here are two examples taken from actual cases: A union had a dispute with a shipping company and it wanted to picket a ship. However, the ship was docked at a privately owned dock. When the dock's owner refused to let the union picket alongside the ship, the union picketed the entrance to the dock. The NLRB ruled that this was not illegal secondary picketing because the four above conditions were fulfilled. In another case, a unionized contractor subcontracted construction work to a nonunion subcontractor. The unionized workers picketed the site, and nobody would work except the nonunion employees. This caused the general contractor to dismiss the nonunion subcontractor. Here the Supreme Court held that the picketing was illegal because the subcontractor's contract was cancelled.[29] Finally, suppose an employer sets up a separate gate or entrance for a group of workers at a multiemployer work site. Another group of workers picket the site. Can they picket the separate gate, assuming our four conditions are met? Yes, if the work done by those who use the separate entrance is closely related to the basic operation of the employer. No, if this is not the case. In the words of the Supreme Court:

> There must be a separate gate, marked and set apart from other gates; the work done by the men who use the gate must be unrelated to the normal operations of the employer, and the work must be of a kind that would not, if done when the plant were engaged in its regular operations, necessitate curtailing those operations.[30]

This implies that picketing a separate gate at a construction site would most likely be illegal, with the exception, of course, that those for whom the gate is set up may themselves picket it.

Question 37: *When can a union use a boycott to put pressure on an employer?*

Generally speaking, a boycott is simply a refusal to use, buy, or deal with some product or some person. There are two types of boycotts: primary and secondary. If General Motors' employees refuse to buy GM cars, this is a primary boycott. The same would be true if A&P workers refuse to patronize the company's stores. In a secondary boycott, workers try to put pressure on a secondary employer (any employer other than their own) or secondary workers or the general public in order to ultimately put the heat on their own employer. There are many types of secondary boycotts, and usually they involve some sort of secondary picketing or striking. Here are some examples:

1) GM workers picket the workplaces of GM's suppliers (glass or tire plants, for example). The purpose of the picketing is to force a work stoppage at the suppliers' plants (which happens when the suppliers' workers refuse to cross the picket line) and thereby put economic pressure on GM which needs the supplies.

2) Food is delivered to A&P by truck drivers who work for an independent trucking company. Any attempt by A&P workers, other than a primary picket line at the A&P store, to force the truck drivers not to make deliveries, would most likely be a secondary boycott.

3) A construction site employs workers of several subcontractors. Striking electricians picket the site (this is called common situs picketing; see Q36) and as a result the subcontractors' employees stop working. Under most circumstances, this is a secondary boycott. It would definitely be one if the electrician's employer has set up a separate entrance for the electricians and they still picket the entire site.

4) A construction company uses nonunion labor. The construction unions in the area then order their members to refuse to work for any employer who does business with the nonunion employer. This is a secondary boycott.

5) J.P. Stevens' workers picket a department store carrying signs urging customers to stop patronizing the store because it carries J.P. Stevens' products. This is an example of a secondary consumer boycott because it is directed at consumers of a secondary employer.

6) In the above situation, the pickets carry signs and pass out leaflets urging customers not to buy J.P. Stevens' products. This is also a secondary consumer boycott.

Of the above six examples, only the last one describes a situation which is clearly legal. Virtually all secondary boycotts are illegal according to the Taft-Hartley and Landrum-Griffin amendments to the National Labor Relations Act. Only secondary consumer boycotts aimed at the product of the *primary* employer are legal. You can ask people not to buy your employer's product but not to stop patronizing a store that sells it. Even here, though, if you picket it must be at a public place (sidewalk, street, etc.).

The law on secondary boycotts is complex and vague, so the NLRB and the courts decide legality on a case-by-case basis. If your primary strike and/or picketing have incidental secondary effects, that is, you do not specifically go after secondary employers, then probably no secondary boycott exists. Striking truck drivers can follow their employers' trucks and picket the delivery areas and probably not engage in a secondary boycott even if the picketing has a harmful economic effect upon the secondary employer. However, four conditions have to hold:

> The picketing must clearly indicate that the union's dispute is not with the person on whose premises it is taking place; it must be limited to times when the struck employer is working on the neutral's premises; it must be limited to places "reasonably close" to the struck employer's activities; and the struck employer must be engaged in his normal business on the premises.[31]

Please note that all of the above refers to workers covered by the National Labor Relations Act. All other workers, except federal government employees, are covered by state laws. Not all states specifically prohibit secondary boycotts, but even those which do not can still use the "common law" to outlaw secondary boycotts. Also note that if you engage in a secondary boycott, the NLRB must seek a preliminary injunction even before it is proven that your actions are illegal. In addition, your union can be sued by employers for economic loss caused by the boycott.

Question 38: *Can we legally refuse to handle "struck work," that is, materials or products sent to our plant from a plant whose workers are on strike?*

Generally speaking, no. What this would amount to is pressure upon your employer to force another employer to agree to the demands of its workers. This is secondary activity (a form of secondary boycott) and is illegal under the Taft-Hartley Act. Contract clauses by which an employer agrees to not require its workers to handle struck goods or penalize them for refusing to do so are called "hot cargo" clauses and were made illegal by the Landrum-Griffin Act.

The exception to the above is when your employer is a very close "ally" of the struck employer. A secondary employer is characterized as an "ally" of the struck firm when:

> (1) a secondary employer performs farmed-out work of a primary employer which would not be done in the absence of a strike; or (2) the secondary employer is so closely identified with the primary employer that they are treated as a single entity or straight line operation.[32]

This "ally" rule is tricky, and you should consult a lawyer before acting. But the above quote does appear to say that if your employer is, in effect, hired by a struck employer to do work ordinarily done by the strikers, you can legally refuse to handle the work. Of course, you should have this right to refuse written into your contract. If not, you may be disciplined for your refusal, and it is doubtful that such a discipline would be itself illegal. If you are not unionized, you must be very careful with sympathy actions or at least be aware of their consequences.

Question 39: *What is a lockout? Are lockouts legal?*

A lockout is a temporary shutdown of a plant by an employer, to discourage unionization or to win demands in bargaining. A lockout to discourage unionization is illegal because it violates Section 7 of the NLRA. However, a lockout used as a bargaining tactic is not, generally speaking, illegal. This type of lockout can be either defensive or offensive. A defensive lockout is one used in response to a strike. For example, suppose that several employers bargain as a multi-employer unit with a single union. The union strikes just one of the employers. In response, the other employers lock out their employees. This is legal. Furthermore, it would very likely be legal for these employers to also hire scabs to replace the locked-out workers.[33] An offensive lockout is one which occurs before or in anticipation of a strike or other concerted activity by workers, the aim of which is to improve the employer's bargaining position. In one case, the employer operated shipyards on the Great Lakes, and because the lakes froze over in the winter, did much of its business during the winter months. The union which bargained with this company, by threatening to strike in the winter, could put heavy pressure on the employer to settle contract disputes on their terms. Therefore, to combat the unions' strength, the company locked the workers out in August, after the employees had rejected the company's last offer, but before a strike. The Supreme Court ruled that this was a legal lockout.[34]

H. Unions and Their Members

The following questions examine the legal rights of union members with respect to their unions. On some occasions it may be necessary for union members to sue their unions. For example, the reform movement in the United Mine Workers which ousted Tony Boyle was helped greatly by winning a suit which overturned Boyle's election as president of the union. However, such suits are complicated and may create tremendous problems within a union.

It may be better for workers to struggle within their unions to reform them from within. Legal proceedings could then be used when other methods of reform have failed, or are not possible to begin with.

Question 40: *Can a union expel a member who scabs? Can a union expel a member for any reason?*

Unions are free to establish by-law or constitutional provisions which define the requirements which the members must fulfill to be in good standing. It can then expel members who are not in good standing. However, there are restrictions on the kinds of good-standing requirements which unions can legally make. The union also must have procedures for expelling members which meet minimum legal standards.

The NLRA is silent for the most part on the internal affairs of unions. However, it does specifically state that the only grounds for which a union can compel an employer to dismiss a union employee is if that employee does not pay his/her union dues and if there is a union or agency shop provision in the contract. This means that a union is free to expel a member according to its constitutional provisions (for scabbing, for refusing to picket, for filing a decertification petition, for defaming the union, etc.), but the expulsion will not result in the expelled member's loss of employment in a union or agency shop, unless the reason for the expulsion is nonpayment of dues. A good feature of this section of the NLRA [Section 8(b)(2)] is that it prevents a union from denying persons employment simply by refusing to admit them or by expelling them in a union or agency shop situation. A bad feature of the provision is that it allows an employee to actively undermine the union without having to fear loss of employment if he/she is kicked out of the union.

A union cannot establish good-standing requirements which violate the laws of the nation. Thus it cannot expel members or deny them admittance because they are black or female or because they have filed unfair labor practice charges against their union. Members would also be protected from expulsion for filing charges under the Landrum-Griffin Act. The Landrum-Griffin Act would also deny a union the right to expel a member who chose to run for office against an incumbent.

Union constitutions usually spell out the internal procedures which are to be followed before a member can be expelled. Every union member should have a copy of the union constitution and be thoroughly familiar with what it says. If your union violates its own procedures in an expulsion (or any other) case, the aggrieved union member may be able to sue the union in a state court. The services of a competent labor lawyer will be needed to do this. The Landrum-Griffin Act (more formally called the Labor Management Reporting and Disclosure Act) itself, in Title I, does guarantee that a union must utilize minimum safeguards in its internal judicial proceedings (expulsion trials, appeals, etc) Charges against a member must be specific and in writing, the accused must be given enough time to prepare a defense, and the accused must have a "full and fair hearing." When a union violates this part of Landrum-Griffin, an expelled or otherwise disciplined member must usually exhaust all internal appeal procedures before using Landrum-Griffin to have the discipline revoked. However, if four months have elapsed from the time the internal appeals were begun, a member can, through a lawyer which he/she must hire, sue the union in federal court. If the disciplined member wins in court (not a jury trial, unless he/she is suing for damages resulting from the expulsion), the judge may award legal fees, although this is rare.

For more information on this question and others which involve the relationships between unions and their members, get a copy of *Democratic Rights for Union Members: A Guide to Internal Union Democracy* by H.W. Benson and available for $5.50 from the Association for Union Democracy, Inc., YWCA Bldg., 30 Third Ave., Brooklyn, NY 11217.

Question 41: *Can a union fine its members?*

Yes, subject to the exact same restrictions as for the preceding question. In addition, fines are collectible through suits in state courts. However, fines plus any special assessments cannot be considered as dues for purposes of causing loss of employment to a person who does not pay them and is then expelled from the union.

The Reagan Board is intent on restricting the rights of unions to discipline their members. In June 1984 it ruled that a union member could resign from a union during a strike despite the fact that the union's by-laws prohibited resignations during a strike or fourteen days before a strike begins. Presumably such a provision violates a worker's NLRA Section 7 right not to engage in concerted activity.[35]

Question 42: *Can my union officers raise dues without a membership vote?*

No. The Landrum-Griffin Act's Title I states that a secret ballot vote of the membership (at a special referendum or at a regular membership meeting) must be taken to decide on dues increases and assessments for local unions. Your international union can raise dues or levy assessments on its own, but its actions are valid only until the next convention.

To enforce this right (and all of the others in Title I), you must first exhaust internal union appeals and then, if necessary, sue your union in federal court.

Question 43: *My local never seems to have elections for union offices. Does it have to?*

A union must obey its constitution with respect to elections. In addition it must obey the provisions of Title IV of Landrum-Griffin. These provision are:

a) *Local Unions.* There must be election of officers by secret ballot of the members at least once every three years.

b) *National or International Unions.* There must be election of officers by secret ballot of the members or by a convention of delegates chosen by secret ballot at least once every five years.

c) *Intermediate Union Bodies (system boards, joint boards, joint councils).* There must be a secret ballot election of officers by members or by labor union officers elected by secret ballot who represent those members at least once every four years.

Landrum-Griffin defines a union officer to be "any constitutional officer, any person authorized to perform the functions of president, vice-president, secretary treasurer, or other executive functions of a labor organization, and any member of its executive board." According to this definition, shop stewards and business agents are probably not officers and need not ever have to stand for election unless the union's constitution says so.

Title IV contains many other election provisions. Union members are guaranteed the right to:

a) nominate officers.

b) run for office if they are in good standing. Good standing cannot be defined in an unreasonable manner. A rule which allowed only those members who had attended 90 percent of all membership meetings over the past three years would be illegal.

c) cast one vote in each union election. Elections must be secret ballot elections.

d) receive mailed notice of the election at least fifteen days before the election.

e) distribute campaign literature. A union must show no discrimination in its treatment of candidates. What it does for one candidate (provide mailing lists, distribute literature, etc.), it must do for all candidates. Union newspapers must give "equal time" to all candidates.
   f) have observers at polling places.

While these guarantees look good on paper, their enforcement is another matter. A union member can sue his/her union for violation of Title IV before the election is over. The same procedure is followed as in Title I suits. However, once the election is over, a member must go through the Secretary of Labor to have an election overturned for violation of Title IV. This is a long and complicated process for which you will need a skilled attorney. A copy of the Benson book mentioned in Q40 would be very useful. In any event, even if you have a good case, the chances of winning a new election are not very good.

Question 44: *What are the procedures for having a union decertified? Is decertification ever a good idea?*

The NLRA contains several provisions which relate to decertification. First, no election, including a decertification election, must have occurred during twelve months preceding the decertification elections [Section 9(a)(3)]. This means that a newly certified union cannot be decertified for at least twelve months.

Second, to get a union decertified, 30 percent of the members of the bargaining unit must sign decertification petitions (available from the NLRB). At a decertification hearing, the NLRB will decide whether or not these are grounds for a decertification election (30 percent interest is generally sufficient) and will, if there are such grounds, call a decertification election. Fifty percent plus one of the members voting in the election must vote to decertify the union if it is to be decertified. The employer can aggressively campaign in favor of decertification.

Third, if your collective bargaining agreement is currently in effect, you generally cannot petition for a decertification election until 90 days before the contract's expiration date.

Care must be taken in any decertification attempt. It may be that even a bad union is better than no union at all. If you simply have your union decertified without having another union replace it, you will be stuck with no union at all for at least one year. However, another union can intervene in the hearing if it can show sufficient interest among the members (30 percent signing authorization cards). Then in the decertification election, two unions plus "no union" will appear on the ballot. If the new union gets a majority of the votes cast, it will be your new bargaining unit. So, before trying to have your present union decertified, make sure that you have another one ready to take its place. Also, remember that AFL-CIO unions have "no raiding" agreements, by which they agree not to raid other unions' members.

Employers have been known to encourage workers to decertify their unions. This may not be illegal if a worker or group of workers initiated the decertification attempt. If you suspect that your employer is behind decertification, file an unfair labor practice change. The NLRB will delay the decertification procedure until the charges are heard and decided.

Question 45: *Is it legal for a union to bar radicals from membership or office?*

Many unions have constitutional provisions which bar communists from membership or office. As of now the higher courts have not ruled on the legality of such clauses, although parts of federal *laws* which had such a prohibition (Taft-Hartley and Landrum-Griffin) were declared unconstitutional. In May of 1981, a court magistrate in Providence, Rhode Island, held that a provision in the by-laws of a carpenter's union local which ordered prospective members to state their political views was illegal. In this case, a potential member had to swear that he was "not affiliated with and never will join or give aid, comfort, or support to any revolutionary organization." The judge ruled that this violated the member's constitutional rights. The local is appealing the decision so it will be a while before a higher court makes a decision.

Question 46: *Can a candidate for union office accept campaign contributions from persons who are not members of the union?*

Yes, unless the union's constitution prohibits such contributions. In a 1982 ruling, the Supreme Court declared that such a provision in the constitution of the United Steel Workers of America did not violate the Landrum-Griffin Act. Ed Sadlowski in 1972 had run unsuccessfully for the USW presidency, and, in the campaign, had solicited money from progressives outside of the union who supported his militant rank-and-file program. After his defeat, the union leadership, fearful of future Sadlowskis, amended the union's constitution with the following clause: "No candidate (in a union election) or supporter of a candidate may solicit or accept financial support, or any other direct or indirect support of any kind (except an individual's volunteered personal time) from any non-member." The lower courts ruled that this violated the Landrum-Griffin Act's "Bill of Rights" (see Chapter Two), but the Supreme Court, in a five to four vote, said that it was legal.[36]

Question 47: *What is a union's "duty of fair representation"?*

Implicit in the NLRA is a union's obligation to fairly represent its members. A union which, say, discriminates against a member of the bargaining unit because of race or causes an employer to penalize a worker in a way not specified in the contract violates Section 8(b)(1) and 8(6)(2) of the NLRA.

A union member may sue a union under Section 301 of the NLRA for failing to represent him/her fairly, the implication being that a union breaks the contract when it fails to represent those for whom it is the sole bargaining agent. The employer can also be sued. For example, suppose a union fails to process a grievance which has obvious merit. The grievant would sue the employer to win the grievance and the union for failing to represent him/her. The court could apportion damages between the company and the union. However, a union does not have to take a grievance to arbitration to represent grievants fairly; it will be given rather wide latitude to decide which grievances are meritorious and which are not. On the other hand, a union is obligated to investigate the facts of a grievance adequately. Failure to do so may subject it to suit.

Two important cases in this area are *Vaca v. Sipes,* 386 US171 (1967) and *Hines v. Anchor Motor Freight, Inc.* 424 US 554 (1976). Naturally, you will need a good attorney with experience in this area. Your union will not provide you with a lawyer to sue it.

I. Other Workers When Not Covered by the NLRA

Question 48: *Employees of small businesses do not seem to benefit much from the labor laws. What can we do to make sure we have the same rights as other workers?*

Employees in small businesses in interstate commerce are not covered by the NLRA if the businesses do less than the NLRB's minimum amount of business. In addition, many intrastate employers are small (remember, no intrastate business, big or small, is covered by the NLRA). Finally, employees in shops with fewer than fifteen workers are not covered by the Civil Rights Acts of 1964 and 1972.

Given their exclusion from these laws, workers in small shops simply do not and cannot have the same legal rights as other workers. However, there are a couple of things which can increase your power to deal with your employer effectively:

1) *Know your state laws* with respect to organizing, injunctions, wages and hours, and health and safety. These laws may provide you with some minimum protection already. In many cases, if your employer is violating these laws, you can file a complaint without your employer finding out your name. Usually you can contact: *State Department of Labor* for laws with respect to organizing, injunctions, and wages and hours; *Office of your local Congressperson* for information about any laws; *Civil Rights Commission, Department of Human Rights or Fair Employment Practice Commission* for any civil rights matter.

While it is beyond the scope of this book to describe state labor laws in detail, here is some basic information about those laws which apply to workers in intrastate commerce:[37]

—Four states have laws patterned after the Wagner Act. They are Connecticut, Massachusetts, New York, and Rhode Island.

—Thirteen states have laws similar to the Taft-Hartley Act. These are Colorado, Hawaii, Kansas, Minnesota, North Dakota, Oregon, Pennsylvania, South Dakota, Utah, Vermont, West Virginia, and Wisconsin.

—Thirteen states have either laws similar to the Landrum-Griffin Act or provisions in their "little Taft-Hartley laws" which regulate internal union affairs. They are Alabama, Connecticut, Florida, Hawaii, Kansas, Massachusetts, Minnesota, New York, Oregon, South Dakota, Texas, Utah, and Wisconsin.

—Numerous states place restrictions on picketing. Alabama, Arkansas, Colorado, Connecticut, Florida, Hawaii, Illinois, Kansas, Michigan, North Dakota, and South Dakota prohibit picketing of homes. Louisiana and Massachusetts bar picketing of courts. Eighteen states do not allow blocking plant entrances or mass picketing: Arkansas, Colorado, Florida, Georgia, Hawaii, Illinois, Kansas, Maine, Michigan, Mississippi, Nebraska, New Mexico, North Dakota, South Carolina, South Dakota, Texas, Utah, Virginia, and Wisconsin.

—Sixteen states regulate or forbid the recruitment of replacements for strikers: California, Delaware, Hawaii, Illinois, Iowa, Louisiana, Maine, Maryland, Massachusetts, Michigan, Minnesota, New Jersey, Oklahoma, Pennsylvania, Rhode Island, and Washington.

2) *Choose a union carefully.* If you want to organize a union, look around for a union willing and able to service a small local. Some unions may not have the resources to service a lot of small locals. Try to locate small shops in your line of work (or any small shop if this is not possible) which are unionized. Ask the workers about the union. Are they happy with it? Does it give them adequate time and help in grievances, strikes, etc.?

3) *Try to bargain informally with your employer.* Many employers are willing to set up informal grievance and safety committees if approached properly. You can use such committees to press for better conditions and possibly as a springboard for a union.

Question 49: *What are the NLRB's minimum "volume of business" standards which it uses to decide whether interstate employers are going to be covered by the NLRA?*

1) *Retail business*—$500,000 gross volume of business.

2) *Non-retail*—$50,000 of goods or services purchased from outside the state or $50,000 sold outside the state.

3) *Public utilities*—$250,000 gross volume.

4) *Transit systems*—$250,000 gross volume.

5) *Newspapers*—$200,000 gross volume plus more than local advertising.

6) *Hotels and motels*—$500,000 gross revenue.

7) *Radio and television stations*—$100,000 gross volume.

8) *Health care institutions*—$250,000 gross volume

It is not that important for workers to know these and your employer won't tell you. You must petition the NLRB for a certification election and let it decide. Your union's legal staff can do the necessary legwork.

Question 50: *In states where public employees cannot legally strike, how are bargaining disputes settled?*

Usually by some type of binding arbitration. Here is a summary taken from Kevin J. Corcoran and Diane Kitell, "Binding Arbitration Laws for State and Municipal Workers," *Monthly Labor Review,* Vol. 104, No. 10 (Oct.1978), pp. 36-40:

Alaska (1972)—All police, fire, and hospital workers must yield to binding arbitration. If other public workers strike, their strike can be enjoined, but the judge can order arbitration. Mediation must precede arbitration.

Connecticut (1975)—All public workers except teachers are covered. Fact-finding and mediation must come before arbitration. The arbitrator must choose the "final offer" of either labor or management on each issue which is unresolved. For example, if the union has last offered a 50 cents per hour raise and management offered a 42 cents per hour raise, the arbitrator must impose 50 cents or 42 cents, but no other number, as the raise.

Iowa (1974)—All public employees are covered, and the two parties can choose how they want to resolve impasses (except by strike!). Factfinding and mediation are mandatory. Final offer arbitration on each issue is used, but if both sides agree, the fact finder's report can be used as the final offer on all issues.

Maine (1974)—County workers are excluded. Factfinding may be requested by labor or management. The arbitrator's ruling is only binding on noneconomic matters. This means that management has the final say on wages and fringe benefits.

Massachusetts (1974)—Here only police and fire fighters are covered by the arbitration law. A government appointed committee decides what form the arbitration takes (single person or board). Arbitration is final offer, but the whole bargaining package of one of the sides, rather than single issues, must be chosen by the arbitrator.

Michigan (1969)—The law covers police, fire fighters, and emergency medical personnel. Final offer arbitration is used for economic issues, but conventional arbitration is used for all other matters.

Minnesota (1969)—In Minnesota public employees have the right to strike except for "essential workers." Regular arbitration is used for these employees. Other public workers can ask for arbitration or strike if the employer won't arbitrate or disregards the arbitrator's ruling.

Nebraska (1974)—Three-judge panels appointed by the governor decide unresolved issues for all public workers.

Nevada (1975)—All local public workers are covered. Mediation is mandatory and factfinding can be binding if both parties agree. Traditional arbitration is used except for fire fighters who must use final offer arbitration on the whole package.

New Jersey (1977)—Police, fire fighters, and prison officers are covered. The parties can choose the form and the type of arbitration. If they cannot agree, final offer arbitration on the package is used for all economic matters, and final offer by issue is used for noneconomic issues.

New York (1974)—Only state police and fire fighters are covered. Regular arbitration is utilized. New York City has its own arbitration law (1972) which mandates that an impasse panel chosen by the City Board of Collective Bargaining mediates disputes and the Board arbitrates. Note that New York's Taylor law covers other employees, with different impasse resolutions.

Oregon (1973)—Nonessential workers can strike or arbitrate; police, fire fighters, mental hospital, and correctional workers must arbitrate. Conventional arbitration is used.

Pennsylvania (1968)—Police and fire fighters can request conventional arbitration after 30 days of bargaining, as can their employers.

Rhode Island—Here there are five different arbitration laws, each covering a different group of workers. For police and fire fighters all unresolved items must go to arbitration after 30 days.

Washington (1974)—Only fire fighters, county police, and police in cities with more than 15,000 persons are covered. After 45 days of bargaining, mediation, factfinding and then conventional arbitration take place.

Wisconsin (1972, 1977)—Basically, all local government employees except police and fire fighters can strike if one party withdraws its final offer. Workers must give ten days notice before striking. Otherwise final offer (package) arbitration is used. Either conventional or final offer (package) arbitration is mandatory for police and fire fighters.

Wyoming (1968)—Fire fighters only are covered and must submit unresolved disputes after 30 days to conventional arbitration.

Question 51: *Are NLRB precedents usually followed in cases involving public employers?*

Yes, unless the federal or state laws which govern the public employees have provisions different than those in the National Labor Relations Act. For example, a strike by federal employees is an unfair labor practice, but this is not true for workers covered by the NLRA. Therefore, the Federal Labor Relations Authority (FLRA) which oversees labor relations for federal workers would react in an entirely different manner in a strike case than would the NLRB. The NLRB would not get involved in a strike at all unless the strike involved some violation of the NLRA. On the other hand, many of the employer actions which the NLRB has declared to be unfair labor practices have also been declared unfair labor practices by the FLRA and by state public employee labor relations boards. Examples include: public employers refusing to let workers wear union buttons; discriminating against workers for union activity; interrogating workers privately about their union sentiments; etc. In such cases the FLRA and state boards almost always use NLRB and court rulings in making their decisions.

J. Other Problems:
1. Civil Rights

Question 52: *Can an employer force employees or job applicants to take a lie detector test?*[38] *What about drug testing?*

More and more companies are requesting job applicants as well as current workers to take lie detector tests. As a result, thousands of applicants are denied employment and many employees lose their jobs because the lie detector tells the employer that they are dishonest or pro-union or homosexuals or smoke marijuana, etc. Lie detectors are not nearly as scientific as their proponents claim and therefore they inaccurately mark many people (perhaps as high as 35-40 percent) who take the tests as liars when in fact they were telling the truth. Sometimes employers provide test results to other employers, in effect blacklisting workers who "failed" the test.

Even if lie detectors were perfectly accurate, they are a massive invasion of privacy. Employers often ask questions totally unrelated to ability to perform the job, such as questions about political beliefs, sexual preference, and union activity.

There is no federal law outlawing or regulating the use of lie detectors. However, the states have begun to regulate the use of polygraphs. At present, eleven states prohibit lie detectors (though usually with exceptions for some employees, especially police); twenty-one states require that tests be voluntary; and nine demand that the tests be administered by licensed professionals.

If your employer demands that you take a lie detector test, here are some possible courses of action:

1) If you are in a union, it is clearly illegal for the employer to institute polygraph testing without first informing and bargaining with the union. The use of polygraphs for current employees is a *mandatory* bargaining subject. It may be difficult, though, for a union to win a contract provision outlawing the use of tests for job applicants because matters involving job applicants are considered by the NLRB to be *permissive* bargaining subjects. As we know, the employer can legally refuse to bargain about such subjects. It is probably illegal for an employer to ask job applicants questions about their attitudes toward unions, but the questions may be so indirect that it would be hard to prove that refusal to answer was "protected activity" under Section 7 of the NLRA.

2) Whether you are in a union or not, if your employer disciplines you for refusing to take a lie detector test or because of the results of a test, you may have some legal recourse. In the states which have made testing illegal or voluntary, you may be able to sue your employer for wrongful discharge in violation of public policy. In a state which allows voluntary testing, you should not agree to be tested. If you do, then any employer discipline may be allowed to stand. If your state has outlawed testing, then you may be able to sue even if you have signed a release prior to taking a test.[39]

3) Whether or not your state has polygraph legislation, you still may be able to sue your employer for wrongful discharge, though your chances of success vary from state to state. Employees have won cases on grounds that the testing involved the "intentional infliction of emotional distress"; "negligent infliction of emotional distress"; "invasion of privacy"; "unreliability of the tests"; etc.[40] It is important to understand that, absent union protection, most employees are employees at will (see Q67) and can be disciplined for any legal reason, including in many states refusal to take a lie detector test.

Some of what has been said about lie detectors could also be said about mandatory drug testing. Drug testing is a mandatory bargaining subject. Public employees do have some Constitutional protection against testing, on the grounds that such testing violates Constitutional demands for due process and prohibitions against unreasonable searches. Private sector nonunion workers enjoy very little protection because there are very few states or local laws which prohibit or regulate drug testing. An exception is San Francisco which has a law which seeks "to protect employees against unreasonable inquiry and investigation into off-the-job conduct, associations and activities not directly related to the actual performance of job responsibilities."[41]

Question 53: *Give us an example of a good "no discrimination" clause.*

Here is one taken from a very good book called *Bargaining for Equality*. (This book deals with sexual discrimination but it can be used for all types of discrimination. You can get it for $5.00 from Women's Labor Project, Box 6520, San Francisco CA 94101):

> The Employer agrees that there will be no discrimination against any employee or prospective employee by reason of age, race, creed, color, national origin, political or religious views, sex or sexual orientation, marital status, appearance or whether she/he has children.

To make sure that this clause covers any employer practice which is not discriminatory on its face but which might have an adverse effect upon some minority, the book recommends a clause like this:

> No employer policy or practice shall have an adverse impact on any groups of employees or prospective employees who are protected under the no discrimination clause.

Question 54: *How can we use the Executive Orders which outlaw discrimination by government contractors?*

The Executive Orders are numbered 11246 (1965) and 11375 (1967). To find out if you are covered, contact your union or the Office of Federal Contract Compliance Programs (OFCCP), Employment Standards Administration, U.S. Department of Labor, 200 Constitution Ave., NW, Washington DC 20210.

Not only do the Orders prohibit discrimination on the basis of race, sex, color, religion, or national origin, they also demand that contractors develop affirmative action programs. This applies to *all* of the contractor's facilities and not just those which actually supply the government. Basically an employer must develop a specific plan for hiring minorities who are underrepresented in its workplaces. It used to be that local labor markets were used for comparison. For example, if Job A had 5 percent women but in the area 30 percent of the local female labor force could do the job, then women were not adequately represented. For *construction* contractors, specific percentages of some minorities had to be achieved by certain dates (6.9 percent women employees by March 31, 1981). However, the Reagan administration has weakened these Orders by ruling that an employer has to maintain these percentages for overall operations and *not* at each individual workplace as was previously the case.

The Reagan administration has done many other things to weaken the Executive Orders, going so far as to suppress two of its own studies which showed that the Orders have resulted in substantial employment and earnings gains for minority and female workers. The OFCCP budget has been drastically cut; compliance reviews have dropped by nearly 40 percent; back pay awards have dwindled significantly; the targeting of specific industries for compliance reviews has been eliminated; and employers have been given the right to monitor their own compliance.[42]

If you think your employer is discriminating, call or write the OFCCP for the detailed regulations which your employer must follow. Then you can file a formal complaint. The OFCCP may then investigate, but you will probably have to bug them. If discrimination is found, the OFCCP will meet with your employer and try to settle the issue. Conceivably the agency can cancel contracts or even keep your employer from getting future contracts. Unfortunately, you cannot sue your employer for violating the law. (Note: this answer was taken from *Bargaining for Equality*, pp. 16-19; see Q53 for details on this book.)

Question 55: *What exactly should I do if I believe that I am being discriminated against because I am a member of a racial minority?*

There are several things which you can do. One approach is to try to end the discrimination by using your union contract. If your contract has a "no discrimination" clause in it, you can file a grievance when this clause is violated by your employer. If it is your union which is discriminating, you can still file a grievance against the employer (who may reap the gains of discrimination), but you can also file an unfair labor practice against the union. Again, first fight within your union for an end to discrimination if at all possible.

Using your contract or filing an unfair labor practice is probably not the best approach to take. The NLRA as well as the Railway Labor Act and state labor laws were not written to attack racial discrimination, and therefore the NLRB and the courts will not always or even usually award you the relief you deserve. So a better approach is to begin proceedings under the various civil rights laws. These proceedings are too complicated to describe briefly, but your first step is to contact the nearest "Equal Employment Opportunity Commission" or "Fair Employment Practices Commission or Agency." Most states and many cities have such commissions, and the federal government has one also. You can find the phone number and address under the local, state, or federal government listings in your phone book. If you have any trouble, consult your union and/or call the local NAACP or other civil rights organization (e.g. American Civil Liberties Union). Once you have made the appropriate initial contact, you will have to fill out a form describing the nature of the discrimination you have suffered, who caused the discrimination, etc. Be sure to include as much and as detailed information as possible at this stage because it may be difficult to amend your complaint later. Get other workers to back you up if you can. After the complaint is made, the local, state, or federal agency will investigate your charge by contacting your employer (or union). An attempt may be made to settle the matter informally at this point. You do *not* have to agree to an informal settlement. If no settlement is reached after 60 days, your case is taken over by the Federal Equal Employment Opportunity Commission (EEOC). If EEOC finds a violation, it makes a ruling ordering the employer to stop discriminating and it also may order back pay, reinstatement, etc. If the employer does not comply with the ruling, the EEOC can sue in federal court. The courts then can fashion their own remedies, but they will probably give weight to the EEOC's ruling. Be prepared for a long wait for a ruling.

Using the EEOC does not prevent you from suing your employer directly. You must wait 180 days after the EEOC gets your complaint and acquire a "right to sue" letter from the EEOC. However, you will have to pay the legal costs yourself. Make sure you get a lawyer with expertise in civil rights law. Also, because the EEOC has a large backlog of cases, it may not help you, or it may try to get you to settle for less than what you are entitled to. You may be better off doing this than waiting forever for a trial.

There are a couple of other things you must remember when filing a Civil Rights Act (or Title VII) complaint. First the federal Civil Rights Acts only apply to workplaces with fifteen or more employees. If you work in a smaller shop, you may be covered by your state law. Check with the state agencies mentioned above. Second, file your complaint quickly. It must be filed with the EEOC within *180 days* of the discrimination (possible 240 days if your state has a fair employment practice agency).

Question 56: *Give us some more specific examples of discrimination that is illegal under the Civil Rights Acts.*

1) Laying off minority workers with more seniority than non-minorities.

2) Asking minority applicants questions not asked of non-minority applicants.

3) Refusing to promote minorities or using standards for promotion (or hiring) which result in disproportionately fewer promotions (or hiring) of minorities.

4) Refusing to hire or promote a woman because women in general may be less capable of doing a particular job (e.g. lifting heavy weights).

5) Refusing to give any benefit to a woman because she is pregnant (assuming that the benefit is given to other employees).

6) A union's refusal to try to end discriminatory practices through collective bargaining. Say that a negotiated pension plan discriminates against some minority. The union is legally bound to try to change this provision.

Question 57: *Give us some details on the Weber decision. What does it mean for minority workers?*

Weber was a white employee of Kaiser Aluminum Company. The company and his union (United Steel Workers) worked out an affirmative action plan in which an in-plant craft training program was established to increase the percentage of black craft workers to the percentage of black workers in the local labor market. To do this, workers were admitted to the craft program from two separate seniority lists, one for whites and one for blacks. Then, workers were chosen from the two lists on a one-for-one basis, one black worker for every white worker. Since plant seniority was the result of past discrimination, whites had the highest plant seniority. This meant that under the plan, some black applicants with less plant seniority than white applicants were admitted to the program. Weber said that this was "reverse discrimination." The Supreme Court said it wasn't. *Weber* is significant because such plans are now legal ways to attack discrimination (of any kind).

Question 58: *What exactly are the legal rights of pregnant workers?*

This answer is again taken from *Bargaining for Equality* (see Q53). I strongly urge all women workers (and certainly all shop stewards) to buy this book. Not only does it describe all the labor laws which affect women, but it has invaluable suggestions for using collective bargaining to fight discrimination, and includes a good list of resources for women workers.

The general rule for pregnant employees is this: your employer cannot deny you *any* benefits or rights because you are pregnant *if* such benefits are available to other employees. This includes hiring, transfer, promotion, leaves of absence, disability payments, medical insurance benefits (except abortion which does not have to be covered by health plans), seniority, etc. If other workers are normally granted leaves for travel or study, etc., then you must be given a similar leave for childcare if you ask for one. This applies to fathers as well. If other workers can transfer to less demanding jobs when they return to work from an illness, you must given the same right when you go back to work after pregnancy. You cannot be forced to take a leave (or quit) because you are pregnant unless being pregnant means that you cannot do your job safely or efficiently.

An important case was decided by the Supreme Court in January 1987. A California law grants special leave privileges for pregnant workers, specifically that they have the right to get their jobs back after their pregnancy. An employer challenged the law, saying that it granted to women privileges not granted to men and therefore violates the federal civil rights laws. Some progressive organizations (NOW, ACLU) have sided with employers arguing that protective legislation has historically worked against women by keeping them out of certain occupations. On the other hand, it is only women who become pregnant and who must usually bear much a child's early nurturing responsibilities. Therefore a good case can be made that, at least until we win job protection for all workers and an equal rights amendment, pregnant women do deserve special protection. The Supreme Court agreed, with Justice Marshall arguing that the state law did not violate the Civil Rights Act because "the act was intended only to provide a base, a minimum standard of treatment for all workers. If states choose to provide additional benefits to pregnant workers, that is not in violation of the law."[43]

Question 59: *I am a working woman, and I am being sexually harassed at work. Do I have any legal protection? What should I do?*

First, get some help right away. There are women's groups in many areas, some of which deal specifically with sexual harassment. Try the National Organization for Women (NOW) or a local women's center. At the very least, you will get a sympathetic hearing and discover that you are not alone. Sexual harassment at work is epidemic in this country.

A list of organizations working on various aspects of sexual harassment was compiled in an excellent pamphlet: *Stopping Sexual Harassment: A Handbook* by Elissa Clarke, available for $2.50 plus .50 postage from Labor Education and Research project, P.O. Box 20001, Detroit MI 48220. I strongly recommend every steward to get a copy of this valuable resource.

You do have legal rights, but they are limited and difficult to enforce. If you decide to take legal action, keep accurate records of all instances of sexual harassment. Try to get witnesses to sign your records and agree to testify in your behalf. Try to locate other women at your workplace who have been sexually harassed. Perhaps a group litigation is possible. Go through all "in-house" grievance channels before filing suit. This insures that the employer cannot say that the harassment was solely the responsibility of the harasser and not the company's fault. Use local women's groups to help you to locate a sympathetic attorney.

Depending on the circumstances of your case, the following legal remedies may be available to you (this is drawn from the Clarke pamphlet):

a) If you are in a union and your contract has a no discrimination clause, you may be able to use it as the basis for filing a grievance for sexual harassment. Arbitrators have awarded reinstatement and back pay to women who have been sexually harassed. However, an arbitrator may not interpret the no discrimination clause to cover sexual harassment. This is one reason why it is a good idea for workers to fight for contract language dealing specifically with sexual harassment. Here is a good one won by a UAW local at Boston University:

> The University recognizes that no employee shall be subject to sexual harassment. In this spirit it agrees to post in all work areas a statement of its commitment to this principle. Reference to sexual harassment includes any sexual attention that is unwanted. In the case of such harassment, an employee may pursue the grievance procedure for redress. Grievances under this Article will be processed in an expedited manner. If, after the grievance is settled, the employee feels unable to return to his/her job, the employee shall be entitled to transfer to an equivalent position at the same salary and grade if a vacancy then exists for which he/she is qualified.

b) If you are in a union, but it will not process your grievance or does so half-heartedly, you may be able to use internal union appeals to get the union to respond. Check your union constitution and follow its procedures carefully. Try to find a sympathetic union official to help you. If you have a strong case (plus some support from coworkers) and your union is really stonewalling, you can file an unfair labor practice charge against it with the NLRB (if you are covered by the NLRA). You would charge it with violating its duty to represent fairly all of its member (see Q47). This is a risky and difficult strategy, and it does not go directly after the harasser. But it may embarrass the union into taking some action.

c) Whether or not you are a union member, you can use the Civil Rights Acts to fight sexual harassment. The EEOC now considers sexual harassment to be a discriminatory act, and the Supreme Court has concurred.[44] To pursue this channel, contact the nearest EEOC office, which may be listed in the phone book under "State Agencies" as a Human Relations or Civil Rights department. In conjunction with the EEOC or privately you can sue your employer for violating the civil rights laws. Some cases have been won, but again it isn't easy to win, especially if the harassment is subtle and you haven't actually been fired or transferred or something similar for refusing to submit to sexual harassment.

d) Some states have civil rights laws, and you may be able to get your case into a state court. Federal law does not provide for jury trials in these cases, but some state laws do. Some state laws also allow compensatory damages (money additional to back pay to compensate the victim for her suffering) which the federal laws do not.

e) If you are harassed by a co-worker, it may not be a good idea to report this to the employer, who is always looking for ways to encourage divisiveness among workers. Instead, first try to deal with the problem more directly, perhaps by seeking support from other workers. If you are in a union, you might be able to get a steward or other officer to deal with your antagonist. You could also, depending on the union's by-laws and constitution, bring the person up on charges of "conduct unbecoming of a union member."

f) There are other legal possibilities such as civil or criminal suits. For these, read the Clarke pamphlet and see a good lawyer. Also, if you lose or quit your job because of sexual harassment, you might be eligible for unemployment compensation.

Question 60: *How can I use the Equal Pay Act?*

You can file a complaint with the EEOC (see Q55) which enforces this law, or you can sue your employer directly. All suits must be brought within two years of your last unequal paycheck (pay includes *all* compensation, not just wages, e.g. holiday and vacation pay).

The hardest thing to show in complaints is that you do or did "equal work." *Bargaining for Equality* (see Q53) says that "Equal work is work requiring 'substantially equal' (1) skill, (2) effort, (3) responsibility, performed under (4) similar working conditions, and with (5) similar job content. Jobs must satisfy *all* of these five conditions to be considered equal under the EPA."

Question 61: *Are gay workers protected by the Civil Rights Laws?*

No, gay workers are not protected by the Civil Rights laws, and therefore employers can legally discriminate against them. Discrimination against gay people has always been severe in the United States, and in the wake of the AIDS epidemic, homophobia has reached hysteric proportions. A few cities have outlawed employment discrimination against gay employees, but federal and state legislation are badly needed. Union workers can push for no discrimination clauses in their contracts (see the one in Q53), but these will only benefit a small proportion of all gay workers.

2. Management Rights and Plant Closings

Question 62: *How can we prevent or limit our employer's ability to subcontract work?*

Your employer must bargain with your union about subcontracting; it is a mandatory item. Therefore, you can contractually limit subcontracting or even prohibit it altogether, if you can get or compel your employer to agree. However, you *cannot* force your employer to use only certain nonbargaining unit workers to do subcontracted work. For example, miners cannot force the company to use union members from some other local every time it subcontracts work. You cannot demand that the subcontractors themselves use union labor (a specific union or a union in general). The strongest contract language which is legally allowed with respect to a subcontractor's employees would be something like this:

> The employer agrees to refrain from using the services of any person who does not observe the wages, hours, and conditions of employment established by labor unions having jurisdiction over the type of services performed.

Question 63: *What are the most important signs that an employer is planning the shutdown of a plant?*

Here are some "signals" of possible plant closing taken from *Economic Notes*, Vol. 50, No. 3 (March 1982), p. 8:

1) Obsolete or deteriorating physical facilities.
2) Obsolete or deteriorating machinery and equipment.
3) Underutilization of plant capacity.
4) Transfer of the parent plant to a new site.
5) Transfer of key personnel or highly skilled workers to other locations.
6) Recent sale or merger of parent company or plant.
7) Shift of profitable product lines to other locations.
8) Overutilization of plant capacity without room to expand.
9) Reduction or liquidation of inventories.
10) Manufacturing technology at the plant is not "state of the art" or comparable to what competitive companies are using.
11) Decline in demand for a product that the plant produces.
12) Source or supply of raw materials or component parts are changing, dwindling, or moving.
13) Increased competition from foreign imports.
14) Increased transportation costs for moving products.

3. Wages and Hours

Question 64: *How frequently does a worker have to be paid?*

To the best of my knowledge, there are no laws which regulate the frequency with which workers must be paid. However, if an employer fails to pay you for work done, you can sue your employer in state or federal court for payment. Of course, you should consult an attorney first. The only wages which can be collected through the Fair Labor Standards Act are unpaid minimum wages and unpaid overtime.

Question 65: *Does my employer have to give me a certain amount of time for lunch and for rest?*

There are no federal laws which mandate rest and meal breaks. However, in an overtime case, the Fair Labor Standards Act has been interpreted so that meal breaks are counted as hours worked if the employee is not relieved of all duties. Similarly, rest periods of twenty minutes or less count as part of hours worked.

While federal laws do not cover breaks, most states have laws which do. You should contact your state Department of Labor or Department of Labor and Industry (look under the "State" listings in your phone book) for details. The department may have a pamphlet which it will send to you.

K. Nonunion Workers

Question 66: *Do the labor laws apply to nonunion as well as to union workers?*

Yes, but some complications exist with respect to the National Labor Relations Act. Section 7 of the NLRA gives workers the right to engage in "concerted" activities. It makes no mention of union membership as a precondition for engaging in collective action. Therefore, nonunion workers ought to be able to do so without being subjected to employer interference. This is clearly the case when nonunion workers are trying to form a union. In fact, in a unionized workplace, a single worker's action, such as refusing to work in an allegedly unsafe workplace, has been held by the NLRB to be "concerted" action, on the grounds that the single worker is in reality acting on everyone's behalf.

But what about "concerted" activity in an unorganized workplace? Here the NLRB and the Supreme Court have agreed that the activities of a group of workers can be protected activity. Thus a group of employees who were fired for leaving work without permission because they believed their plant to be too cold for work were ordered reinstated with back pay. They had spoken to their employers about the cold but to no avail, so they walked out as a last resort. Such behavior, the Court ruled, was "concerted" activity and protected by the NLRA.[45]

However, if a single worker is disciplined for his/her individual behavior (e.g. complaining to a public agency about an unsafe workplace), the NLRB will not consider this behavior to be protected activity.[46] This has not always been the case; before the Reagan Board came to power, the NLRB would have found such action to be protected, although not all of the Appeals Courts agreed.[47]

Question 67: *What is meant by "at-will" employment?*

"At-will" employment is the common law concept, pretty much unique to the United States, which gives an employer the right to fire a worker for any reason at all, that is, at the employer's will. Until very recently, nearly all employees not protected by a union contract were at-will employees. Of course, as we have learned, an employer cannot fire a worker because of that worker's union activity or race, sex, creed, ethnic origin, or age because such discrimination is now against the law. But in all other situations, unless protected by a union contract, most workers could be fired for any reason (e.g. appearance, demeanor, weight, sexual preference, whistle-blowing, etc.) or for no reason at all.

Over the past twenty years or so, however, some courts have weakened the at-will doctrine and ordered fired workers in certain cases to be reinstated. These are complicated cases, and you will need a good lawyer to pursue a challenge to the at-will doctrine. At least three exceptions to at-will have been recognized by *some* courts.[48] First, if you are dismissed for upholding a public policy by, for example, refusing to disobey a law when ordered to do so by your employer, you may have a case. Second, you might challenge your discharge if you can show that you were fired because of your employer's malice, bad faith, or retaliation. Here the argument is that good faith behavior is implied in each employment contract. Third, you might argue that you had an implied promise of job security and/or due process in your employment contract.

Chapter 6 _____

LABOR LAW REFORM

In this book I have tried to explain the labor laws so that the average worker can understand them and use them effectively. If we know our rights and how to enforce them, then we will be better able to meet the daily attacks made upon us by our employers. While the NLRB and the courts are hardly the champions of the working classes, they do sometimes give workers an opportunity to move their struggles forward. When the laws give workers rights, the NLRB and the courts cannot simply ignore them. Knowledgeable workers know this and use the legal system to their maximum advantage.

The labor laws of the United States do protect workers to a certain extent, but as preceding chapters have made clear, there is much room for improvement. Compared to many other industrialized capitalist nations, the U.S. gives its workers minimal protection. Our labor laws do not adequately address a host of very serious problems: racial discrimination, sexual discrimination, health and safety, plant closings, forced overtime, poverty-level wages, and employer refusal-to-bargain, not to mention the Taft-Hartley restrictions described in Chapters Two and Five. Enforcement of the laws which do exist is often weak and arbitrary. There is no doubt, therefore, that we must have better labor laws and these must be adequately enforced. Labor law reform has to be high on the action agenda of the labor movement. The question is: how can we get better labor laws? In this final chapter I try to provide some answers through an examination of two historical experiences. The first is the failure of the AFL-CIO to win minor reforms of Taft-Hartley in 1977. The second is the success of Missouri unions and their allies in defeating a right to work initiative in 1978. From these two case studies, perhaps we can learn some important do's and don'ts of labor law reform.

Having said that we must have more progressive labor laws, I must offer a few words of caution. We live in an economic system in which our workplaces are privately owned and operated strictly to make a profit, and our government's basic function is to defend this system. It is becoming more obvious every day that private profit-making is not compatible with the health, safety, security, and freedom of workers. Only when we control workplaces ourselves will we be able to structure them to meet our needs. Until then the fight has to take place on all fronts, including legislation, but we must remember that no amount of labor law reform will create a free and just society. Labor laws have to be seen as tools which we can utilize in a broader struggle, but not as ends in themselves. Workers in Sweden have better labor laws, but they still suffer from exploitation, unemployment, inflation, and most important, the inability to determine *what* they will produce.

We must also not spend too much time and energy in purely legal struggles. Legal victories are important, but they are time consuming and costly. Many workers have painfully discovered that even when they won in the courts, their unions were already destroyed and they had suffered losses which could never be recovered. Workers are at a distinct disadvantage in almost any legal proceeding, regardless of how good are the labor laws. Any company has more financial and legal resources than any worker, and any really large corporation can outspend any union. In most litigations workers must rely upon the opinion of lawyers and judges instead of their own power to stop the flow of profits by direct actions. The point is that workers cannot liberate themselves through legal reform alone. Legal struggles are necessary but not sufficient.

A. Anatomy of a Failure:
The Labor Law Reform Bill of 1977

As we learned in Chapter Two, the AFL and the CIO vowed in 1947 to fight against the anti-labor Taft-Hartley Amendments. To date, they have been stunningly unsuccessful. The "muscle" of organized labor has failed to prevent passage of the Landrum-Griffin Act and has been unable to win a *situs* picketing law for construction workers. There are more states with "right to work" laws now than there were when Taft-Hartley was passed.

Nowhere was organized labor's relative weakness more clearly revealed than in its failure to lobby passage of the Labor Law Reform Bill through Congress in 1977 and 1978.[1] This bill was successfully filibustered in the Senate by a group of right-wing senators and never actually came to a vote before the entire Senate. The bill's defeat occurred despite one of the AFL-CIO's most intensive lobbying efforts, despite the facts that the President was a Democrat (the so-called party of labor), both houses of Congress were Democratically controlled, and the bill had been endorsed by the President and other leading Democrats.

What went wrong? Was the bill too "radical" to be enacted? Hardly. It was a mild reform which in no way would have turned the tide against Taft-Hartley or seriously hurt most businesses. Its major provisions would have speeded up union representation elections and unfair labor practice decisions, allowed certification if 55 percent of a unit's members had signed authorization cards, increased the size of the NLRB, given unions greater access to employer premises, awarded back pay at time and one-half for workers illegally discharged for union activity, and provided for monetary penalties for employer refusal-to-bargain. This last provision might have proven expensive to some employers, but it has to be put into the context of the sharp increase in the number of employers who have simply ignored their duty to bargain in good faith. Basically, all that the reform bill would have done was give some teeth to the rapidly deteriorating enforcement of already existing labor laws. The really anti-labor provisions of Taft-Hartley such as right to work, secondary boycotts, free speech, and injunctions would have remained intact.

Though the bill itself was not very progressive, could it have been that "public opinion" had become so conservative that Congress could not risk passing any labor law reforms? This argument too does not stand up to close scrutiny. While it sometimes seems that public hostility toward unions (and especially union leaders) is increasing, researchers have found upon careful analysis that one out of three unorganized workers would like to become union members, and most workers approve of unions in principle. Specifically, a 1979 *Monthly Labor Review* survey [2] reported that: "between 60 and 70 percent of Americans approve of unions in general and of the rights of workers to join unions." And, "more than 80 percent of the respondents agreed that unions improve the wages and job security of their members and represent their members against unfair labor practices of employers." Further, on a wide range of social issues such as health insurance and aid to the poor and the cities, pollsters have found average citizens to be fairly liberal.

It must be admitted, however, that politicians do not ordinarily respond to "public opinion" unless it is organized in such a
way that failure to respond would be costly to them. Perhaps
people do support unions and labor law reform, but for this support
to mean anything it must be organized politically. The reason why
the Labor Law Reform Bill failed is simple: labor did not mobilize
enough union members and sympathetic elements of the general
public in support of the bill, while labor's enemies engaged in an
unprecedented lobbying effort to defeat it.

Labor lobbied strongly, but its methods were ineffective.
Through its political arm, COPE (Committee on Political Education), the AFL-CIO sent its lobbyists into Congress to twist the
arms of labor's "friends," in the traditional manner of "you
support us here and we'll support you for reelection or on some
other issue." Legislators were contacted and lots of money was
spent, but the bill never got out of Committee.

Organized labor failed to do the one thing which all politicians
must respect—aggressively organize and mobilize the politicians'
constituents. It did not adequately educate union members and
labor's potential allies about the need for better labor laws. There
were articles in union newspapers but very little face-to-face shop
floor and door-to-door education. Without this basic grassroots
organizing, it was not possible to generate millions of telephone
calls and telegrams to legislators or to conduct massive demonstrations, work slowdowns, nationwide one-day strikes, and so
forth to show politicians just how serious labor was. Why should a
politician just take a labor lobbyist's word for it that support for a
bill will help the politician and refusal to support it will be
dangerous? Unless the lobbyist's word is backed up by numbers of
vocal, educated workers and allies, it cannot compel legislators to
pay attention.

While labor was lobbying in Washington, business was
organizing everywhere. Since World War II, employers have
developed sophisticated organizations to influence public opinion
as well as local, state, and federal legislation.[3] Hundreds of
thousands of relatively small employers are organized into groups
such as the National Federation of Independent Business, National Association of Manufacturers, U.S. Chamber of Commerce,
Associated Builders and Contractors, and the Associated General
Contractors. Giant businesses have formed the Business Council
and the Business Roundtable. There are also employer supported
"single issue" groups such as the National Right to Work Committee (NRWC) and the National Action Committee on Labor Law
Reform. In the past, many of the big multinationals, with long
histories of relationships with unions, had refused to aggressively

and openly attack the labor movement figuring that such action might push the AFL-CIO toward more militant and radical bargaining and politics. However, given the recent absence of a fighting stance by the labor movement and its shrinking hold on the U.S. labor force, a large number of these multinational giants joined forces with smaller employers to oppose the Labor Law Reform Bill, believing that there was little labor could do to them.

Employers, therefore, were united in their opposition to the bill. What is more, they did not rely solely upon their professional lobbyists. Instead, they systematically built up a tremendous groundswell of local and regional hostility to the bill. Using mailing lists produced by right-wing publicity wizard Richard Viguerie, employer groups mailed millions of pieces of anti-reform literature to known and potential allies. These people were encouraged to let their elected officials know that they were opposed to the bill. Then, in the words of a recent *Nation* magazine article, "As the bill moved toward a vote on the Senate floor, lobbying and bargaining were intense. Plane loads of businessmen flooded Washington (and) business launched a nationwide press campaign of canned editorials and advertising..." General Electric Company even "sent plant managers to lobby against the bill at the height of the debate."[4] The National Right to Work Committee mailed out an astounding fifty million postcards attacking the bill; six million of these were returned to members of Congress. Ultimately the bill was filibustered to death in the Senate, and some Republicans who wanted to vote to end the filibuster were kept in line by the fear that the NRWC would send out mailings attacking them.

B. Anatomy of a Success:
The Missouri "Right to Work" Initiative

The disastrous Labor Law Reform Bill campaign demonstrated the difficulties with the AFL-CIO's national lobbying tactics. Continuing use of these tactics will mean future failures to win political victories for workers. Worse still, now that we are saddled with the aggressively reactionary, anti-labor Reagan administration and a thoroughly pro-business Congress, the labor victories of the past are being rolled back. Already there is considerable sentiment in Washington to enact a federal right to work law; OSHA has been gutted; black lung and mine safety enforcement have diminished; many unions are actually afraid to go before the NLRB. Unless labor changes its ways, it is probable that workers will suffer continuous setbacks.

How specifically should labor respond? One way to find out is to examine a labor victory and see what strategies proved successful.[5] In 1978, voters in Missouri defeated by a wide margin a referendum which would have made Missouri a right to work state. The voting took place on November 7, 1978. Little more than a year before, polls indicated that nearly two-thirds of all Missouri voters favored a right to work law. Unbelievably, 40 percent of all union households favored it. The petitions necessary to get a right to work amendment to Missouri's constitution on the November ballot were completed by July 1978, just four months before the voting. Organized labor began its campaign to defeat the amendment in December 1977, but did not really begin to move until about two and one-half months before the election. Therefore, in just ten weeks, labor was able to completely reverse the trend shown by the early polls. A potential debacle was converted into a smashing victory. How did this happen? Can what happened in Missouri be repeated in other states and at the national level?

Before we analyze the Missouri anti-right to work campaign, some background on right to work will be useful. As we know, a right to work law forbids unions the right to negotiate a union shop with an employer, even if the employer agrees to one. Therefore, with a right to work law, no one has to join the union after it has been certified despite the fact that it *must* bargain for and represent *all* of the workers in the bargaining unit. In most right to work states, the only form of union security which is legal is the open shop, which is no security at all.

In an open shop, not all workers will belong to the union. Since nonmembers receive all of the benefits of any union contract, there is not much of an incentive for some workers to join the union, weakening its financial strength. Where nonmembers can "free-load" from the union members, there is bound to be hostility within the work force, which management can exacerbate by subtly favoring nonmembers with better work assignments or promotions. Management could, in fact, hire new workers known to be hostile to the union, and when there are enough nonmembers it could persuade some of them to try to get the union decertified. Nonmembers could actively undermine the union by continually slandering it or crossing its picket lines without having to worry about union discipline.

The right to work movement in Missouri was part of a larger anti-union movement led by the National Right to Work Committee (NRWC). The NRWC was founded in 1954 by Fred Hartley (of Taft-Hartley infamy) and right-wing industrialist E.S. Dillard. Today it takes in over $8 million per year in contributions (mostly from businesses), files dozens of lawsuits against unions, aggressively and effectively promotes right-wing political candidates, and lobbies for right to work laws at both the state and national levels.

NRWC, in turn, is part of a network of right-wing and anti-labor organizations which include the National Association of Manufacturers, the Chamber of Commerce, the U.S. Industrial Council and hundreds of other local, state, and national organizations. Many of these are of recent origin, but similar groups have existed since the "open shop" movement of the early 1900s. This movement reached its peak in the 1920s when labor union membership fell to record low levels. With the passage of the Wagner Act, anti-labor groups were temporarily put on the defensive. But as we pointed out in Chapter Two, they soon recovered and went on the offensive again. Because labor was relatively strong nationally, labor's enemies intensified their state-level activities. The phrase "right to work" was coined by a Dallas newspaperman in 1941 and has been the rallying cry of unionbusters ever since. It is an ingenious phrase because although it is completely misleading (right to work laws guarantee no one the right to work), it is very appealing to people in a country with high average unemployment rates.

Florida was the first state in which the right to workers were successful. A right to work law became part of Florida's constitution in 1944. Since then, nineteen other states have enacted right to work laws: Alabama, Arizona, Arkansas, Georgia, Iowa, Kansas, Louisiana, Mississippi, Nebraska, Nevada, North Carolina, North Dakota, South Carolina, South Dakota, Tennessee, Texas, Utah, Virginia, and Wyoming. All of these states have outlawed union shops; most of them have banned agency shops as well; and a few have placed restrictions upon dues check offs.[6]

These states are largely in the South, a region in which workers have long suffered from lower wages, less adequate fringe benefits, and poorer social services than workers in the rest of the country. Right to work laws have contributed significantly to the region's failure to catch up with economic conditions elsewhere despite a massive movement of industry into right to work states. Regardless of what statistic you use, workers in right to work states are worse off than workers in "free" states ("free" states will mean those without right to work laws): fewer of them are in unions; their wages are lower; the average income for everyone is lower in their states; they have fewer protections (e.g. minimum wage, overtime pay, equal pay for women; sex, race, and age anti-discrimination laws) and enjoy fewer and inferior social services.[7]

As you can see, right to work states are not exactly paradises for workers. However, right to work laws hurt all workers because they help to maintain the low wages which attract runaway shops from heavily unionized states. Only by making all states "free" states can labor hope to improve its lot everywhere. This is why the fight against right to work is so important, and this is what gave the Missouri struggle extra significance. Missouri was in most respects not at all similar to the RTW states. In 1978 it was the eighth most heavily industrialized state in the country; its two major cities, St. Louis and Kansas City, were important centers of aircraft, automobile, chemicals, alcohol, and food production. Lead and coal mining were also large industries. Many large corporations were headquartered in Missouri: Annheuser-Busch, Chromalloy, McDonnell-Douglas, 7-Up, Monsanto, Ralston-Purina, Pet Inc., and others. Matching the power of business was a large and historically militant labor movement. St. Louis especially had long been known for its activist unions; the Teamsters, for example, had built a progressive and socially conscious union under the leadership of Harold Gibbons. Overall, more than one-third of Missouri's nonagricultural labor force were in labor unions making it the tenth most unionized state in the United States.

Despite Missouri's union history, state right to work leaders believed with good reason that it was ripe for right to work. Beneath the surface of heavy industry and strong unions were many favorable conditions. Missouri's labor movement was badly divided, with no central leadership, and with frequent power struggles and in-fighting. This made labor politically weak. It could usually defeat hostile legislation in the state legislature, but it could not push through progressive laws. Outside of St. Louis and Kansas City, there was a large and conservative rural population which right to work forces felt they could count on for support. Other support could be won by those concerned with the exodus and threatened moves of businesses from Missouri to the five surrounding right to work states. Finally, the country as a whole seemed to be moving right, a lot more pro-business and anti-labor in attitude. RTW leaders hoped to capitalize on such attitudes in Missouri and to strengthen them by widely publicizing instances of union corruption and lack of democracy.

Given the many splits in the ranks of labor, union leaders were slow to respond to the right to work threat. A "United Labor Committee" (ULC) had been formed in 1973 to defeat an earlier right to work bill in the legislature. ULC continued to exist but did not really mobilize until after RTW's successful petition drive in 1978. In Kansas City, a "Right to Truth Committee" had been organized in 1975, and it was more active in exposing the lies of right to work, but it existed only in one city. Right to work's strategy was to introduce a bill in the state legislature, knowing it would fail, but hoping to get wide exposure for their ideas. After the bill was beaten, they would initiate a petition drive to get a right to work constitutional amendment on the ballot for voters in November 1978.

This plan worked smoothly, but its success failed to stir labor. Many leaders believed that the right to work petitions would not be validated by the State Attorney General because of the widespread fraud which was used to get signatures on the petitions. However, the Attorney General did validate the petitions in late August. In the meantime, ULC filed suit in state court to have the petitions declared invalid. A time consuming and costly legal battle took up almost the entire month of August. In one sense the lawsuit helped labor because the publicity it generated won some labor support. Yet, on balance, it probably did more harm than good. Labor leaders thought that the suit would be won, and most of them refused to activate the massive campaign needed to defeat RTW. When the judges ruled against the suit, there was precious little time to wage war against the right, which had long since begun to put its campaign into high gear.

Once labor realized that right to work would be on the ballot and had an excellent chance of winning, labor leaders, spurred by their more conscious rank-and-file, sprang into action. The ULC, which had more or less spearheaded the anti-right to work movement from the beginning, continued to do so, only on a more planned and unified basis. Gradually, a three-pronged strategy was developed based upon: "1) voter registration, get-out-the-vote, and rank-and-file action; 2) communications (mass media, direct mail, and phone banks); and 3) coalition building."[8] In March the ULC had commissioned a poll which indicated that once people knew what RTW was, they were much more likely to be opposed to it. Throughout the petition campaign ULC and various local unions organized an educational campaign with speakers' bureaus, debate in the media, articles in labor newspapers, bumper-stickers, and buttons. The slogan "Right to Work is a Ripoff" was created and became labor's major educational message.

In August, ULC hired consultants Matt Reese and Associates and a data bank corporation, Claritas. Reese engineered the voter registration campaign and helped to organize the media campaign and the coalition building. Voter registration (less than one-half of Missouri's union members were registered to vote) and get-out-the-vote efforts were based upon the concept of multiple contacts—by phone, by mail, and in person and then repeating in various sequences. Another survey was taken in September which showed that RTW was losing ground. On the basis of this survey, new educational materials were developed for the multiple contacts.

To effectuate the voter registration and the get-out-the-vote campaigns, phone banks were developed with the help of the unions and some sophisticated use of computer technology. Union members were contacted first, and many of them became actively involved in the campaign as a result of these contacts, helping to develop a strong rank-and-file effort. But to get at the nonunion voters, whose votes were needed to win, ULC relied upon data collected by Claritas and the polls taken earlier. Claritas keeps detailed socio-economic data for people in over 300,000 small geographic areas which it calls "block groups." Each block group contains about 280 families who have tended to react similarly to marketing techniques. Then, in the words of UAW district director Ken Worley:

> Poll data on the RTW issue was overlaid and correlated with the Claritas block groups, allowing projection of survey results down to each county, ward, precinct or block group in Missouri. For the first time, it was possible to identify very small groups of voters "leaning toward" opposition to RTW, or "persuadable." Using a Claritas computer coding system, some of the key groups included:
>
> —low to middle income ethnic urban blue collar
> —low income city and urban fringe blue collar
> —low income to poverty rural farm (white)
> —middle income suburban blue collar
>
> Voters in each "cluster" group could be targeted for mail and phone contact anywhere in the state, while avoiding neighbors who were likely supporters of RTW.

Altogether Reese constructed a list of 590,000 "target" names, that is, people most likely to be favorable or leaning towards the anti-right-to-work side. Some 366,000 persons were actually contacted and 360,000 homes visited, one of the results of which was the recruitment of 24,000 volunteer workers. The basic idea was to contact only those people who either definitely were likely to vote against right to work or who could be persuaded to do so, while purposely ignoring others. Reese believed that if pro-right to work people were ignored, there was less chance that they would vote. Many unionists, especially rank-and-filers in clusters which were ignored, were upset by this decision. Some simply ignored it, worked hard in what were supposedly right to work strongholds, and in some cases, succeeded in winning majority votes against right to work. What this proves is not that the Reese approach was wrong but that the key to labor success is an aroused rank-and-file.

The ULC communications program, which used data already collected by the polling, was set up by two sympathetic Kansas City public relations/advertising executives who left their jobs to work against right to work. Six weeks before the vote, they set up

"ADhoc" to handle all "copy, art, production, broadcast and print media, and some public relations." ADhoc, in turn, was advised by a task force from AFL-CIO and international unions and drew on them for public relations and media professionals. In about five weeks, ADhoc "did more than 100 separate jobs—close to 9 million pieces of literature." Again, the communications were targeted to the sympathetic cluster areas, for example, advertisements only in those newspapers or on those radio and television stations most likely to be used by targeted people and least likely to be used by pro-RTW voters. Not only was this approach successful, but it also saved a lot of money.

Mass mailings, phone banks, voter registration, and communications, all combined with the use of "outside specialists" and computer technology, were important to the success of the anti-right to work struggle. However, what really tipped the scale in labor's favor was a successful campaign to build coalitions with natural allies. Too often in the past, labor (and not just in Missouri) had not sought help from the broad progressive community; at times it was even hostile to it. Labor leadership in Missouri had opposed an anti-nuclear referendum and supported a dam project opposed by environmentalists. But as a later analysis revealed, union members had in large numbers voted with labor's alleged "enemies." Had leaders taken the time to listen to their members and not been afraid to mobilize them, the labor movement could have forged powerful coalitions with a variety of groups.

Right to work was such a threat to labor, however, that a few clearsighted union leaders and many members realized that without organized support from outside of the labor movement, right to work could not be beaten. Eventually, ULC developed plans to seek the support of the religious community, farmers, students, the women's movement, senior citizens, environmentalists, and consumers. To get the coalitions rolling, a general ULC meeting, open to all locals in the state, was held on October 17. Important potential supporting organizations were represented; Senator Edward Kennedy gave a strong speech blasting right to work; and several groups came out against it. Over 2000 persons attended the meeting, mostly local union members. After the meeting, they went back to their communities and actively lobbied their pastors, store owners, parents (many of whom were farmers), and others to vote "no."

The coalitions were remarkably successful. Labor discovered that just about everybody in Missouri except big business had an interest in defeating right to work. It was just a matter of developing the right educational materials for each group and then making sure that they got the message. For example, many of Missouri's farmers have small holdings and sell most of their crops locally. If wages are low then their sales will suffer, so these farmers really have a stake in a unionized, high-wage economy. Even if farm laborers were organized, these farmers' costs would be unaffected because they hire very few employees. By making the connection between the earnings of small farmers and right to work, ULC was able to win strong support from them. ULC emphasized face-to-face contacts with farmers, often through their children who were union members in the cities. In addition, labor won support from the militant farm organizations, the American Agricultural Movement (AAM) and the National Farmers Organization. Support from the AAM came easily because some unions, notably the United Mine Workers and the Teamsters, had already built cordial relationships with it. AAM had helped the miners during their long strike in 1977 and the Teamsters lent a helping hand to AAM during its nationwide protests the same year.

Coalitions with other groups were built in much the same way, although these were more dependent upon soliciting important leaders from these groups to speak out against right to work. Blacks rallied overwhelmingly to labor's cause; both state and national civil rights leaders went out of their way to win votes in the black communities. Black people suffer in every state in the country, but they are bound to be relatively worse off where wages and working conditions are poorest. Black workers need a strong and progressive labor movement, and it was in their direct interests to vote against right to work. However, black workers had many grievances against organized labor, which often gave lip service to civil rights but seldom delivered the goods. Many black citizens wondered why their leaders were working so hard for labor when labor had done so little for them. As one person put it, "During the campaign, we'd go into economically depressed areas and they'd ask us, why you knocking yourself out for them creeps." Ultimately, black people saw the need to defeat right to work and voted almost unanimously against it. But they will expect something from the labor movement in return. Hopefully they will get it, but labor got off to a bad start by playing "Dixie" at labor headquarters the night of the victory.

The result of labor's "triple threat" campaign against RTW was a resounding victory. Over 190,000 new voters were registered; 100,000 of these were union members. Voter turnout set an off-election year record, and 100,000 more votes were cast on the RTW amendment than in the political races. The vote against right to work was significantly higher in the cluster groups than elsewhere, giving partial vindication to the Reese/Claritas technique. Most importantly, with the exception of students, all of the coalition groups voted with labor. Students probably voted for right to work because of the notable pro-business bias of most school curriculums and teachers, but also perhaps because when students get part-time or summer jobs with unionized companies, the unions are mainly interested in their dues money and represent them poorly.

C. The Lessons of the Two Campaigns

In the Labor Law Reform Bill campaign, organized labor utilized tactics which it had used many times before, but which had never worked very well unless labor was operating from a position of strength. Today, as in the 1920s, labor is weak politically both because its membership is declining and because what members it does have are seldom mobilized by the leadership, for reasons that I will develop below. But even given labor's relative powerlessness, the Missouri campaign demonstrated that the labor movement can still organize effectively to defeat its enemies. It further demonstrated that to do so requires that at least three things be done. First, labor must use "outside" expertise and modern media and public relations technology. The right can get literally millions of pieces of mail to members of Congress on short notice; there is no reason why labor cannot do the same. The right has managed to manipulate the media to get a large number of ignorant and mean-spirited people elected to the highest offices in the land; surely labor could use media more skillfully to help to get decent progressives elected. Second, labor must build coalitions with its many potential friends, including those with whom it does not always agree. Environmentalists, peace and anti-nuclear advocates, and consumers all benefit form a strong labor movement. By the same token, workers want a clean environment, a peaceful world, and safe, high quality products. Labor has common interests with many groups and must seek them out, actively support them whenever possible, and work toward permanent coalitions.

Third, and most critically, labor's rank-and-file must be aroused to participate and help to lead in the struggle for labor law reform and general progressive social change. History shows clearly that labor does best when employers and the government fear an aggressive, militant rank-and-file. Without the marches, strikes, and factory occupations, the Wagner Act would not have been passed in the 1930s. Without massive participation and leadership by local union members, right to work would not have been defeated in Missouri. Only workers can make the face-to-face contacts essential for building a grassroots progressive movement in the United States.

Is there hope that the lessons of Missouri will be learned? At the present time, I do not think that it is possible to say. Right now, the labor movement in the United States appears weaker relative to capital than at any time since the Great Depression. Unions are winning a smaller percentage of representation elections and being decertified more often than at any time since the passage of the Wagner Act. Employers are asking for and getting large give-backs which eat away at gains which took many years to win. The Reagan administration is orchestrating an anti-worker campaign more vicious than anything since the 1920s. Civil rights, health and safety, unemployment compensation, public assistance, job and social security programs—all of these and more are being systematically dismantled under Reagan. To make matters worse, the government has rushed headlong into an insane military buildup, greatly increasing the risk of the ultimate catastrophe, nuclear holocaust.

In the face of all this, organized labor has not yet gotten its bearings. It is relying too much upon its old tactics of lobbying and working within the Democratic Party. It is too much on the defensive. What it must do is to get aggressive; it must develop a progressive, anti-corporate, and popular program and ideology of its own. And it must work tirelessly to get its message across to the people and to build coalitions with its natural allies. The Right has shown clearly that masses of people can be motivated to act because they believe in something. The labor movement and all progressives must learn this lesson from the Right and act on it. We have the advantage of ideas and policies bound to be more appealing than their narrow and selfish platform.

Already we see signs of popular resistance to Reagan's assault upon the working class: the Solidarity Day rally in Washington DC in September 1981; the rebirth of the peace movement; growing protests and demonstrations by the poor; and the formation of organizations of the unemployed.[9] More resistance is bound to occur in the future, and the labor movement will assume its natural leadership role in it. Just as in the 1930s the CIO became the leader of all progressive forces, so too can the labor movement of today rise up and seize the opportunity to build the just and humane society of the future.

Chapter 7 _____

Glossary

Here are definitions of many of the terms used in this book. They are arranged alphabetically for convenient reference.

Affirmative Action: Actions taken by an employer to improve the employment situation of minorities. This is required of employers with government contracts, and it is sometimes ordered by EEOC and the courts in civil rights lawsuits.

Age Discrimination in Employment Act (ADEA): Law passed in 1967 which prohibits discrimination against people 40-70 years old. It is administered by the EEOC.

Agency Shop: A form of union security in which workers do not have to join the union which is their bargaining agent, but all workers must pay dues.

Alter-Ego Employer: A type of successorship in which the successor employer is, in fact, the same as the employer which it has succeeded.

Arbitration: A method of settling grievance disputes and sometimes used to settle bargaining disputes (usually for public employees). A person called an arbitrator is chosen and given the power to make a binding decision to resolve the dispute. An arbitrator's decision cannot usually be appealed.

At-Will Employment. The common law doctrine which states that an employer may discharge an employee for any reason, that is, at the employer's will.

Authorization Cards: Cards signed by workers who want to organize a union. They indicate that the workers want a union. The NLRB and state labor agencies usually require that 30 percent of the proposed bargaining unit sign cards before an election will be held.

Bad-Faith Bargaining: Occurs when an employer (or a union) refuses to bargain seriously. It is an unfair labor practice under the NLRA.

Bargaining Unit: Those workers making up a union to bargain with their employer.

Bill of Rights: The first 10 Amendments to the Constitution guaranteeing that the government will not interfere with our basic freedoms—speech, assembly, religion, etc.

Bona Fide Occupational Qualification (BFOQ): Under the Civil Rights Acts (and the Age Discrimination in Employment Act) an employer cannot use sex, race, age, religion, or national origin as job qualifications unless they are absolutely essential (bona fide) for the job's performance. The burden of proof is on the employer.

Boycott: Refusal to deal with some employer. In a *primary boycott* workers refuse to work for, handle, or buy the product of their employer. In a *secondary boycott*, workers try to get other employers or the general public to stop dealing with their employer. Most secondary boycotts are illegal.

Certification Election: An election conducted by the NLRB or some state or federal labor agency to see if workers want to be represented by a union. If the union wins, it is legally *certified* as the bargaining agent for the workers.

Civil Rights Act of 1866: A civil rights law recently used by *black* workers to fight against employment discrimination. It only applies to *racial* discrimination.

Civil Rights Acts of 1964 and 1972: These are the most important civil rights laws. They make discrimination by race, sex, religion, and national origin illegal.

Closed Shop: A form of union security in which *only* members can be hired. It is illegal under the Taft-Hartley Amendments to the NLRA.

Common Law: Laws made by judges not legislatures. Where there are no statutes or written laws, the common law is used. It is not usually very favorable to labor unions. Common Law is the only labor law for intrastate commerce in states with no written labor laws.

Common Situs Picketing: Picketing by a union at a work site where more than one group of employees is working. It usually occurs at construction sites and is usually illegal if it causes the other workers to stop working. (It is then a form of secondary boycott.)

Company Union: A union formed by or dominated by an employer. It implies an unfair labor practice under the NLRA if formed to keep workers from establishing their own union.

Concerted Activity: When workers join together to protect themselves or to win their demands, they are engaging in concerted activity.

Consent Decree: A decree in which two sides agree to something before the issue goes to court. Consent decrees are common in civil rights and health lawsuits. If you or your union agree to a consent decree then ordinarily you give up your right to sue.

Conspiracy Doctrine: The idea that unions are illegal because they are conspiracies. A conspiracy is a plan by two or more persons to injure a third party. This doctrine is no longer applied to unions.

Cost-Benefit Standard: Standard proposed by industry in OSHA cases. Before an OSHA regulation could be put into effect, OSHA would have to show that the "benefits" outweigh the "costs" to industry.

Decertification Elections: An election to decide whether workers want to get rid of (decertify) their union.

Department of Labor: Federal Government agency involved in many labor laws, especially Civil Rights Laws, Fair Labor Standards Act, and the Landrum-Griffin Act. The Department of Labor is located at 200 Constitution Ave. NW, Washington DC 20210.

Disparate Impact: Term used in discrimination cases to describe an employment practice which, while not obviously discriminatory, results in reduced employment opportunities for minorities. For example, a requirement that an employee must be six feet tall to get a certain job is not discriminatory on the surface, but it would exclude most women. Therefore it has a "disparate impact" upon women, and is illegal unless absolutely necessary for performance of the job.

Disparate Treatment: Term used in discrimination cases to describe an employment practice which treats minorities differently than nonminorities.

Due Process: Before the government can interfere with your Constitutional rights, you must be given due process, for example, the right to a court hearing, appeals, etc.

Duty of Fair Representation: The duty of a union, implicit in the NLRA, to adequately represent the members of the bargaining unit.

Economic Strikers: Workers who strike for better wages, hours, or working conditions. Economic strikers do not have automatic reinstatement rights.

Employment Retirement Income Security Act (ERISA): Act passed by Congress in 1974 to reform pension abuses.

Enjoined: If you are under an injunction order, you are said to be "enjoined."

Equal Employment Opportunity Commission (EEOC): The EEOC administers the Civil Rights Acts of 1964 and 1972, the Age Discrimination in Employment Act, and the Equal Pay Act. Their address is: US Equal Employment Opportunity Commission, Washington DC 20506.

Equal Pay Act: This law guarantees women "equal pay for equal work." It is administered by the EEOC.

Equal Rights Amendment (ERA): A proposed Amendment to the Constitution guaranteeing equal rights for women.

Executive Orders: Orders issued by the President or a state or city executive which regulate unionization and collective bargaining for certain public employees or employees who work for government contractors. They are like labor laws except that they are not passed by Congress or a legislature and can be changed at the executive's discretion.

Factfinding: This occurs almost always with public employees when there is a collective bargaining impasse. A factfinder is appointed according to specific legal procedures to investigate the impasse. The factfinder then issues a report (a factfinding) which can be made public. The idea is to put pressure on the two sides to settle. The factfinder has no power to settle the dispute.

Fair Employment Practices Commissions: These are state agencies which hear and investigate discrimination complaints. They work with the EEOC.

Fair Labor Standards Act: Federal law passed in 1939 to set minimum wages and overtime rules and to regulate child labor. It is administered by the Wage and Hour Administrator of the US Department of Labor.

Final Offer Arbitration: A form of arbitration in which the arbitrator must choose the last offer of the union or the employer. This decision is then imposed upon both sides. In *final offer/package arbitration*, this is done for an entire bargaining proposal. In *final offer/issue arbitration* this is done only for unresolved bargaining issues.

Free Speech: The "free speech" provision of the Taft-Hartley Amendments to the NLRA, in Section 8(c), allows employers much more freedom to actively combat unions than did the original Act.

Funded Pension: A pension plan for which money has been set aside in advance to pay the pensions.

Hiring Hall: A union security device in which the employer must obtain workers through the union which maintains a hiring hall. Prospective workers must register at the union hall to get employment.

Hot Cargo Clause: A contract provision which allows employees to refuse to handle work produced by an employer whose plant is being struck. It is illegal under the Landrum-Griffin Amendments to the NLRA.

Impasse: A breakdown in collective bargaining.

Injunction: A court order which tells some party (a person, a union, an employer) to stop doing something.

Interstate Commerce: Buying and/or selling across state lines.

Intrastate Commerce: Buying and/or selling strictly within the borders of a single state.

Jurisdictional Strike: A strike resulting from a dispute between two unions over which one is to represent a group of workers. It is illegal under the Taft-Hartley Amendments to the NLRA.

Landrum-Griffin Act: Federal labor law passed in 1959. The major part of it regulates the internal affairs of labor unions, while the rest of it further amends the NLRA. It is also known as the Labor Management Reporting and Disclosure Act.

Lockout: Closing of a plant by an employer to put pressure on workers during negotiations or to keep them from forming a union.

Maintenance of Membership: A weak form of union security in which workers do not have to join the union, but if they do join, they must maintain their membership at least until the contract expires.

Management Rights: Those "rights" which employers claim must be free from worker interference and not subject to collective bargaining.

Mandatory Bargaining Subject: A topic about which the employer must bargain with a union. Examples are wages, hours, and terms and conditions of employment.

Mediation: A method used to try to settle bargaining impasses. The two parties choose a "mediator" whose job it is to get the two sides bargaining again. However, the mediator only gives advice and does not have the power to impose a settlement. Mediation is mandatory for many public employees.

National Emergency Strike: A strike which the President thinks endangers the welfare of the nation. Taft-Hartley gives the President the power to declare that a strike is a "national emergency" and to seek a temporary injunction to stop it for 80 days.

National Labor Relations Act (NLRA): Law passed in 1935 which gave workers in interstate commerce the right to join unions and bargain collectively with their employers.

National Labor Relations Board (NLRB): The board which administers the NLRA.

Norris-LaGuardia Act: Law passed in 1932 to restrict the use of injunctions in labor disputes. It is also known as the Anti-Injunction Act.

Occupational Safety and Health Act (OSHA): Law passed in 1970 to guarantee workers safe and healthy workplaces.

Occupational Safety and Health Administration (OSHA): Body which administers the Occupational Safety and Health Act (also called OSHA). Address: US Department of Labor, Assistant Secretary for Occupational Safety and Health, 200 Constitution Ave. NW, Washington DC 20210.

Office of Federal Contract Compliance (OFCCP): Federal office in the Department of Labor which enforces Executive Orders 11246 and 11375 which prohibit discrimination by government contractors. Address: Office of Federal Contract Compliance Programs, Employment Standards Administration, US Department of Labor, 200 Constitution Ave. NW Washington DC 20210

Open Shop: A unionized workplace in which union membership is not mandatory. States with Right to Work laws are called "Open Shop" states.

Pension Benefit Guarantee Corporation (PBGC): A federal corporation established under ERISA to guarantee certain types of pensions.

Permissive Bargaining Subject: A topic about which the employer can legally refuse to bargain because it is part of "management rights." An example would be the price of the product.

Picketing: Patrolling by workers in front of a workplace to keep strike breakers out and/or to inform the public of a labor dispute. Picketing solely to tell the public something about an employer is called *informational picketing*. Picketing to organize a group of workers is called *organizational picketing*. Picketing by large numbers of workers is called *mass picketing,* and this can be an unfair labor practice.

Portable Pension: A pension plan to which you can belong even when you change employers.

Punitive Damages: Awards made by courts, in addition to reinstatement and back-pay, to punish an employer (or union) for violating the law and to serve as an example to others.

Railway Labor Act: The first national labor law passed in 1926 to guarantee to railroad workers the rights to unionize and to bargain collectively.

Reporters: A general term used to describe the volumes which contain the records of NLRB and court cases.

Right to Work Law: A law which makes the union shop illegal.

RM Petition: A petition for a certification election filed by an employer who has a good faith doubt that the union represents the majority of the employees in the bargaining unit.

Sole Bargaining Agent: The NLRA says that when a union wins a certification election, it becomes the sole (only) legal bargaining agent for all of the employees in the bargaining unit.

Successorship: The transfer (through sale, merger, etc.) of one company to another. An important question is whether the new owner is bound by a contract negotiated by the old owner.

Sympathy Strike: Strike in support of another group of workers. This is usually illegal.

Taft-Hartley Law: Amendments to the NLRA which were extremely anti-union.

Title VII (Civil Rights Acts of 1964 and 1972): The part of the Civil Rights Acts which specifically prohibits employment discrimination.

Unfair Labor Practices: Acts by employers or unions which violate Section 8(a) or Section 8(b) of the NLRA.

Unfair Labor Practice Strikers: Workers on strike to protest an employer's unfair labor practices. Such strikers must be reinstated after the strike.

Union Security: That part of a collective bargaining contract which gives security to the union. Examples are closed shop, union shop, dues checkoff, and hiring hall.

Union Shop: A form of union security in which employees must join the union at some time after they are hired.

Vested Pension: A pension to which you are entitled (usually after some minimum number of years in the plan) even if you stop working under the plan. Of course, if you do not work until retirement age under the plan, your pension payments will be reduced.

Wage and Hour Administrator: Department of Labor official who administers the Fair Labor Standards Act.

Wagner Act: The name given to the original NLRA.

Workers' Compensation Laws: State laws which provide compensation for workers injured or made ill by their jobs.

NOTES

Notes to Chapter One

1. "Union Busters," *Southern Exposure*, Vol. VIII, No. 2 (Summer 1980), p. 29.

2. *Ibid.*, p. 43.

3. Data on the overall membership and membership in particular unions is from "The Deunionization of America," *The Economist*, Vol. 290, No. 7313 (Oct. 29, 1983), p. 77. Data on elections is from Anne Field, "Seceding From the Union," *Forbes*, Vol. 128, No. 9 (Oct. 26, 1981), p. 40. See also Paul Weiler, "Promises to Keep: Securing Workers' Rights to Self-Organization Under the NLRA," *Harvard Law Review*, Vol. 96, No. 8 (June 1980), pp. 1772-1780.

Notes to Chapter Two

1. There are many books which you can read to learn more about labor history and labor laws. Unfortunately, not many of them are written from a worker's point of view and in a readable style. An exception is Philip S. Foner, *History of the American Labor Movement in the United States*, currently 6 volumes and

growing, (New York: International Publishers, various dates). I used these volumes frequently in writing this chapter. Some other books which I used are Marjorie S. Turner, *The Early American Labor Conspiracy Cases* (San Diego: San Diego State College Press, 1967); Charles O. Gregory and Harold A. Katz, *Labor and the Law* (New York: W.W. Norton & Co., 1979); Harry A. Millis and Emily C. Brown, *From the Wagner Act to Taft-Hartley* (Chicago: Chicago University Press, 1950); Robert Justin Goldstein, *Political Repression in Modern America* (New York: Schenkman Publishing Co., Inc., 1978); Richard O. Boyer and Herbert M. Morais, *Labor's Untold Story* (New York: United Electrical, Radio & Machine Workers of America, 1972); David Milton, *The Politics of U.S. Labor* (New York: Monthly Review Press, 1982); and Jeremy Brecher, *Strike!* (Boston: South End Press, 1977).

2. Foner, Vol. 1, p. 157.

3. 4 Metcalf 111 (Mass. 1842). This is a legal reference. I will explain these as we go along. The records of legal cases are kept in bound volumes called "reporters." These reporters can be found in the law libraries of courthouses and universities. The "federal reporters," in which federal court case records are bound, can be found in many libraries, but the "state reporters" may only be in large libraries or in the specific state's courthouse libraries. This reference to *Commonwealth v. Hunt* is unusual because the case occurred before the "reporters" system began. The first number listed—4—is the volume number. "Metcalf" is the name of the actual person who made the report for the case. Usually the name of the court would appear instead. The second number—111—is the page in volume 4 on which the case begins. "Mass. 1842" tells us that this case was heard before the Massachusetts State Supreme Court in 1842. To find this case in a Massachusetts law library you would ask for Volume 4 of the Metcalf Reports. Then just turn to page 111.

4. *Hitchman Coal Co. v. Mitchell*, 245 US 229 (1917). Here the letters—US—tell us that this case was heard by the U.S. Supreme Court. This 1917 case can be found in Volume 245 of these reports on page 229. You could find this case in just about any law library. Also look at Question 1 in Chapter Five for more information on researching labor law.

5. See Gregory & Katz, pp. 83-104, for more on injunctions.

6. Goldstein, p. 56.

7. *Loewe v. Lawlor*, 208 US 274 (1908).

8. *Gompers v. Bucks Stove and Range Co.*, 221 US 418 (1911).

9. *United Leather Workers v. Herkert & Meisel Trunk Co.*, 265 US 457 (1924).

10. *United Mine Workers of America v. Coronado Coal Co.*, 259 US 344 (1925).

11. Foner, Vol. 1, p. 507.

12. The Knights, however, were racist with respect to Chinese. It should also be noted that their ideals and their actions often diverged.

13. A. T. Lane, "American Trade Unions, Mass Immigration and the Literacy Test: 1900—1917," *Labor History*, Vol. 25, No. 1 (Winter 1984), p. 15.

14. Goldstein, p. 114.

15. *ibid*, pp. 103-136.

16. *ibid*, p. 124.

17. *ibid*, p. 122.

18. See Gregory & Katz, pp. 269-279, for details.

19. *School District, City of Holland, Ottawa & Allegan Counties, Michigan v. Holland Education Association.*, (Mich. 1968) 47 Labor Cases 51,874. Here the "Mich." tells us that the Supreme Court of Michigan made this ruling. It is reported in yet another "reporter" called Labor Cases, which is published by Commerce Clearing House. See Question 1 in Chapter 5 for more details.

20. *Senn v. Tile Layers' Protective Union,* 301 US 468 (1937).

21. *New Negro Alliance v. Sanitary Grocery Co.* 303 US 552, 304 US 542 (1938).

22. In the case just cited in footnote 20.

23. See Gregory and Katz, pp. 184-199, for the philosophy of the Norris-LaGuardia Act. The quote is by noted sociologist Robert S. Lynd, cited in Christopher L. Tomlins, "The New Deal, Collective Bargaining, and the Triumph of Industrial Pluralism," *Industrial and Labor Relations Review*, Vol. 39, No. 1 (October 1983), p. 27.

24. On average, it now takes 322 days for the NLRB to rule on an unfair labor practice. If the decision is appealed to the courts, another year will go by (on average) before a decision is reached.

25. *Republic Steel Corporation v. NLRB,* 311 US 7 (1940).

26. *Pennsylvania Greyhound Lines,* 1 NLRB 1 (1935).

27. See Rick Hurd, "New Deal Labor Policy and the Containment of Radical Union Activity," *The Review of Radical Political Economics*, Vol. 8, No. 3 (Fall 1976), pp. 32-44.

28. Tomlines, pp. 29-35.

29. For an excellent discussion of boycotts and the general hostility of Taft-Hartley to labor see Paul Weiler, "Promises to Keep: Securing Workers' Rights to Self-Organization Under the NLRA," *Harvard Law Review*, Vol. 96, No. 8 (June 1980), pp. 1769-1827.

30. *Livingston Shirt Corporation* 107 NLRB 400 (1953). Here the letters—NLRB—tell you that this was an NLRB and not a court decision. The official NLRB "reporter," in this case Volume

107 at page 400, can be found in a law library. Again, see Question 1 in Chapter 5.

31. Weiler, p. 1814.

32. Weiler, pp. 1799-1801.

33. *Gateway Coal Co. v. UMW*, 414 US 368 (1974).

34. *U.S. v. Brown*, 381 US 437 (1965).

35. Unions in health care institutions (hospitals, clinics, nursing homes, etc.) must give a 90 day notice and must submit to mandatory mediation and fact-finding. They must also give a ten day notice before engaging in a strike, picketing, or other concerted activity. Failure to do so is an unfair labor practice.

36. A good illustration of the intra-union struggle between anti-communists and progressives in the United Auto Workers can be found in Martin Halpern, "Taft-Hartley and the Defeat of the Progressive Alternative in the United Auto Workers," *Labor History*, Vol. 27, No. 2 (Spring 1986), pp. 204-226.

37. Data in this paragraph are from Weiler, pp. 1774-1781. Quotation is from Paul Weiler, "Striking a New Balance: Freedom of Contract and the Prospects for Union Representation," *Harvard Law Review*, Vol. 98, No.2 (December 1984), p. 354.

Notes to Chapter Three

1. Of course, many farms in the Midwest are nearly completely mechanized and use few employees, while numerous small farms are run with family labor.

2. There are many good books about farmworkers. An especially good one is Peter Matthiessen, *Sal Si Puedes* (New York: Random House, 1973).

3. For some background on the UFW see Richard W. Hurd, "Organizing the Working Poor—The California Grape Strike Experience," *The Review of Radical Political Economics*, Vol. 6, No. 1 (Spring 1974), pp. 50-75.

4. Karen S. Koziara, " Agricultural Labor Relations Laws in Four States—A Comparison," *Monthly Labor Review,* Vol. 100, No. 5 (May 1974), pp. 14-18.

5. For more on domestic workers see Allyson Shannan Grossman, "Women in Domestic Work: Yesterday and Today," *Monthly Labor Review*, Vol. 103, No. 8 (Aug. 1980), pp. 17-22. The National Committee on Household Employment can be reached at 500 E. 62nd St., New York NY 10021.

6. Actually the NLRB changed its mind a couple of times on this issue. In *Packard Motor Car Co. v. NLRB,* US 485 (1947),

the Supreme Court upheld the NLRB's ruling that supervisors could be employees under the NLRA.

7. *Eastern Greyhound Lines v. NLRB*, 337 F. 2d. 84 (6th Cir. 1963) and *NLRB v. City Yellow Cab*, 344 F. 2d 575 (6th Cir. 1965). Here the symbols "F. 2d" tell us that this case can be found in another reporter, this one called the "Federal Reporter" (the 2 means second series of this reporter). The Federal Appeals Courts are located in various regions or "circuits" of the country. The *Yellow Cab* case was heard in the "6th Circuit" in 1965. As in the other examples the first number—337—is the volume number and the second number—84—is the page number.

8. *Wichita Eagle & Beacon Publishing Co., Inc. v. NLRB*, 480 F. 2d 52 (10th Cir. 1973).

9. *NLRB v. Yeshiva University*, 440 US 906 (1980).

10. Much of this material on the Railway Labor Act is taken from John Schmidman, *Labor Law* (State College, PA.: The Pennsylvania State University, 1981).

11. For discussion of this issue as well as more details on the Railway Labor Act, see Dennis A. Ardula and Henry H. Perritt, Jr., "Transportation Labor Regulation: Is the Railway Labor Act or the National Labor Relations Act the Better Statutory Vehicle?," *Labor Law Journal*, Vol. 36, No. 3 (March 1985), pp. 145-172.

12. For details on all of the NLRB monetary minimums see the book *Labor Law Course* (Chicago: Commerce Clearing House, 1980), pp. 1553-1558.

13. See Charles O. Gregory and Harold A. Katz, *Labor and the Law* (New York: W. W. Norton & Co., 1979), pp. 234-236.

14. Basic information on public employees and their unions can be found in Edwin F. Beal, Edward D. Wickersham, and Philip K. Kienast, *The Practice of Collective Bargaining* (Homewood, Ill.: Richard D. Irwin, Inc., 1976), pp. 447-506; and especially Richard B. Freeman, "Unionism Comes to the Public Sector," *Journal of Economic Literature*, Vol. XXIV, No. 1 (March 1986), pp. 41-86. Most of the data on public employees is taken from the Freeman article.

15. See Stephen C. Shannon, "Work Stoppage in Government: The Postal Strike of 1970," *Monthly Labor Review*, Vol. 104, No. 8 (July 1978), pp. 14-22.

16. Actually postal workers are no longer federal employees; they work for the independent government corporation established when the Post Office was reorganized in 1970. The Postal Reorganization Act makes postal workers subject to Taft-Hartley in union representation and unfair labor practice matters. However, the Postal Reorganization Act itself contains provisions which outlaw strikes, limit union security, and provide for mandatory fact-finding and arbitration.

17. This story was repeated in *The Guardian,* Dec. 8, 1982, p. 2.

18. I got valuable information on how Title VII works from Jeff Lewis, a former organizer for National Federation of Federal Employees.

19. *American Federation of State, County and Municipal Employees, AFL-CIO v. Woodward,* 406 F. 2d 137 (Eighth Cir. 1969).

20. Lynn Zimmer and James Jacobs, "Challenging the Taylor Law: Prison Guards on Strike," *Industrial and Labor Relations Review,* Vol. 34, No. 4 (July 1981), pp. 531-544.

21. *Abood v. Detroit Board of Education,* 431 US 209 (1977).

22. For some interesting advice on public worker unionism, read Paul Johnston, "The Promise of Public Service Unionism," *Monthly Review,* Vol. 30 (Sept. 1978), pp. 1-17.

Notes to Chapter Four

1. *Bessie B. Givhan v. Western Line Consolidated School District,* 439 US 410 (1979).

2. *Pickering v. Board of Education,* 391 US 563 (1968).

3. *NLRB v. Republic Aviation Corp.,* 324 US 793 (1945).

4. *Eastex, Inc. v. NLRB,* 98 US 2505 (1978).

5. A book which deals in depth with the civil rights laws and employment is William B. Gould, *Black Workers in White Unions* (Ithaca, N.Y.: Cornell University Press, 1977). Unfortunately this book is not very easy to understand.

6. *Steel v. Louisville and Nashville Railroad,* 323 US 192 (1944).

7. *Handy Andy Inc.,* 228 NLRB 447 (1977).

8. Michael Reich, *Racial Inequality: A Political Economic Analysis* (Princeton, NJ: Princeton University Press, 1981).

9. *Hughes Tool Co.,* 147 NLRB 1573 (1964).

10. *Emporium Capwell Co. v. Western Addition Community Organization,* 420 US 50 (1975).

11. *Griggs v. Duke Power Co.,* 401 US 424 (1971).

12. *McDonnell Douglas Corp. v. Green,* 411 US 792 (1973).

13. *International Brotherhood of Teamsters v. United States,* 431 US 324 (1977). Also, see *Frank v. Bowman Transportation Co.,* 431 US 324 (1976).

14. The relevant cases are *Memphis Firefighters Local Union No. 1784 v. Scotts,* 104 SC 2576 (1984). *Cleveland Firefighters Local Number 43, International Association of Firefighters AFL-CIO, CLC, v. City of Cleveland,* 478 US (1986); *Local 28 of the*

Sheet Metal Workers' International Association and Local 28, Joint Apprenticeship Committee v. EEOC, 478 US (1986); and *Wendy Wygant v. Jackson Board of Education,* 476 US (1986).

15. *University of California v. Bakke,* 438 US 265 (1978).

16. *United Steel Workers of America v. Weber,* 443 US 193 (1979).

17. See Lewis M. Steel, "Why Attorneys Won't Take Civil Rights Cases," *The Nation,* Vol. 236, No. 12 (March 26, 1983), pp. 302-364.

18. *General Electric Co. v. Gilbert,* 429 US 125 (1976).

19. See *Williams v. Saxbe,* 431 F. Supp. 654 (CA-DC,1976); *Barnes v. Costle,* 561 F. 2d 982 (CA-DC, 1977); *Bundy v. Jackson,* 641 F. 2d 934 (CA-DC, 1981).

20. *County of Washington v. Gunther,* 452 US 161 (1981). See also the June 16, 1981 issue of *Guardian* (newspaper) and Raymond L.Hogler, "Equal Pay, Equal Work, and the United States Supreme Court," *Labor Law Journal,* Vol. 32 No. 11 (Nov. 1981), pp. 737-744.

21. *AFSCME v. State of Washington,* 578 F. Supp. 846 (1983). For a brief review of the case, see *Monthly Labor Review,* Vol. 106, No. 11 (November 1983), p. 75.

22. *AFSCME v. State of Washington,* 770 F. 2d. 1401 (9th Cir., 1985). For a critical analysis of this decision, see Garth Mangum and Stephen Mangum, "Comparable Worth Confusion in the Ninth Circuit," *Labor Law Journal,* Vol. 37, No. 6 (June 1986), pp. 357-365.

23. This section relies upon Gregory & Katz, *Labor and the Law,* pp. 575-579; Gary Goldman, "ADEA's Section 663(b) Defferal Provision: A Trap for Unwary Plantiffs," *Labor Law Journal,* Vol. 34, No. 10 (October 1983), pp. 632-642; and Marvin F. Hill, Jr. and Terry Bishop, "Aging and Employment: The BFOQ Under the ADEA," *Labor Law Journal,* Vol. 34, No. 12 (December 1983), pp. 763-775.

24. There are some exceptions to the Act's coverage, most notably top executives with relatively large pensions.

25. *NLRB v. J. Weingarten, Inc.,* 416 US 969 (1975).

26. This clearly weakens the *Weingarten* doctrine (note 25) because it says an employer can ignore due process if it has "just cause" for a discipline. This would be similar to allowing a suspect's conviction in court to be upheld despite police violation of the Bill of Rights in apprehending the suspect. Incidentally, the Weingarten doctrine only applies to workers covered by a collective bargaining agreement. (See Q66 for rights of unorganized employees.) See *Taracorp,* 273 NLRB 54 (1984) recently upheld by an Appeals court.

27. *NLRB v. Borg-Warner Corp.,* 356 US 342 (1958).

28. *Plastic Transport, Inc.*, 193 NLRB 54 (1971).

29. *First National Maintenance Corp. v. NLRB*, 452 US 666 (1981).

30. *Otis Elevator Company, United Technologies*, 1983-84, 269 NLRB No. 162 (April 6, 1984).

31. Cited in Jeffrey Johnson, "Plant Shut-downs: A Pervasive Problem," *Economic Notes*, Vol. 48, No. 5 (May, 1980), p. 3.

32. The Braniff story was reported in *The Guardian*, December 15, 1982, p. 2.

33. *NLRB v. Bildisco and Bildisco*, 115 LRRM 2805 (1984).

34. The relationship between labor and bankruptcy law is complex, but see Mark S. Pulliam, "The Collision of Labor and Bankruptcy Law: Bildisco and the Legislative Response," *Labor Law Journal*, Vol. 36, No. 7 (July 1985), pp. 390-401.

35. *Burns International Security Services, Inc. v. NLRB*, 406 US 272 (1972), and *Howard Johnson Co. v. Detroit Local Joint Executive Board*, 417 US 249 (1974).

36. See the citation at footnote 30, and Robert H. Bernstein and Richard Cooper, "Labor Law Consequences of the Sale of a Unionized Business," *Labor Law Journal*, Vol. 36, No. 6 (June 1985), pp. 327-336.

37. Bernstein and Cooper, pp. 333-335.

38. Bob Baugh, "Shutdown: Mill Closures and Woodworkers," p. 3. This excellent paper has a lot of information about shutdowns and successorships. I will send you a copy on request.

39. North American Congress on Latin America, "Abandoning Steel: Capital Finds the Better Way," *NACLA Report on the Americas*, Vol. XIII, No. 1 (Jan.-Feb. 1979), p. 13.

40. Mark Green and Norman Waitzman, "The Corporate Attack on Regulation," *URPE Newsletter*, Vol. 12, No. 2 (Mar./Apr. 1980), p. 4.

41. "Anti-OSHA Rationales," *Economic Notes*, Vol. 46, No. 10-11 (Oct.-Nov. 1979), p. 5.

42. A good book on health and safety which I have used here is Daniel M. Berman, *Death on the Job* (New York: Monthly Review Press, 1978).

43. *Gateway Coal Company v. U.M.W.*, 414 US 368 (1974).

44. Berman, p. 141.

45. *Marshall v. Barlow's, Inc.* 429 US 1347 (1978).

46. See Edward H. Greer, "OSHA's Cotton-Dust Standard: Deregulation Fever Hits the Supreme Court," *The Nation*, Vol. 231, No. 21 (Dec. 20, 1980), pp. 666-668.

47. See Lawrence E. Dube, Jr., "OSHA's Hazard Communication Standard: 'Right to Know' Comes to the Workplace," *Labor Law Journal*, Vol. 36, No. 9 (September 1985), pp. 696-701.

48. See Mary P. Lavine, "Industrial Screening Progress for

Workers," *Environment,* Vol. 24, No. 5 (June, 1982) pp. 26-38.

49. OSHA corruption is well-documented in a series of articles written by Jonathan A. Bennett in *The Guardian* during the winter and spring of 1986. "Temperatures Rise in OSHA Scandal," (February 12, 1986, p. 3) and "Publicity is the Biggest Hazard for OSHA Bosses," (February 19, 1986, p. 5) are representative examples.

50. *National League of Cities v. Usery,* 426 US 833 (1976).

51. *Garcia v. San Antonio Metropolitan Transit Authority,* 105 US 1005 (1985).

52. *Inland Steel co. v. NLRB* 170 F. 2d 297 (7th Cir. 1948).

53. This section relies heavily upon Charles O. Gregory and Harold A. Katz, *Labor and the Law* (New York: W.W. Norton and Co., 1979), pp. 628-642.

54. *Allied Chemical and Alkali Workers, Local 1 v. Pittsburgh Plate Glass Co., Chemical Division,* 404 US 157 (1971).

Notes to Chapter Five

1. *United Dairy Farmers Cooperative Association v. National Labor Relations Board,* 633 F.2d 1054 (3d Cir., 1980). For an article which discusses this case and related matters, see George R. Salem, "Non-majority Bargaining Orders: A Prospective View in Light of *Union Dairy Farmers," Labor Law Journal,* Vol. 32, No. 3 (March 1981), pp. 145-157. The decision which permits bargaining orders without elections is *NLRB v. Gissel Packing Co,* 395 US 575 (1969). The NLRB ruling which prohibits such orders under a majority of workers have signed authorization cards is *Gourmet Foods,* 270 NLRB 12 (1984).

2. *Excelsior Underwear Inc.,* 156 NLRB 1236 (1966).

3. *Southwestern Bell Telephone Company v. Communications Workers of America, AFL-CIO,* 200 NLRB 101 (1973).

4. *Peerless Plywood Co,* 107 NLRB 427 (1953).

5. This speech was taken from John Schmidman, *Labor Law* (State College, PA: The Pennsylvania State University, 1981), pp. 17-18.

6. *NLRB v. Babcock and Wilcox Co.,* 351 US 105 (1956). For an article which covers the main issues here (although from an anti-labor viewpoint), see Evan J. Spelfogel, "Private Property Picketing," *Labor Law Journal,* Vol. 33, No. 10 (October 1982), pp. 659-667.

7. See Felicia A. Firston, "The Board's Role in the Arbitral Process," *Labor Law Journal,* Vol. 32, No. 12 (December 1981), pp.

799-807. The Reagan Board decision which abdicated increasing authority to arbitration in *United Technologies Corp*, 268 NLRB 557 (1984).

8. *Textile Workers of America v. Darlington Manufacturing Company*, 380 US 263 (1965).

9. The Reagan Board has greatly increased the power of employers to make fundamental, unilateral changes for "economic" reasons, but it is still an unfair labor practice for an employer to do things out of anti-union hostility.

10. *St. Francis Hospital I*, 265 NLRB 1023 (1982).

11. See Robert A. Swift, *The NLRB and Management Decision Making*, (Philadelphia: Wharton School, 1974) for details on this issue.

12. The NLRB ruled that it did not have the power to award monetary damages in refusal-to-bargain cases in *Ex-Cell-O Corp*, 185 NLRB 20 (1970).

13. Paul Weiler, "Striking a New Balance: Freedom of Contract and the Prospects for Union Representation," *Harvard Law Review*, Vol. 98 No. 2 (December 1984), pp. 354-355.

14. The major cases are known as the "Steelworkers Trilogy." A good discussion of them is in Charles O. Gregory and Harold A. Katz, *Labor and the Law*, (New York: W. W. Norton, 1979), pp. 489-493.

15. On this and related matters, see Frank Elkouri and Edna Asper Elkouri, *How Arbitration Works* (Washington DC: Bureau of National Affairs, 1973), pp. 26-44.

16. See Robert Lewis, "Union Decertification: A New Look at Management's Role," *Labor Law Journal*, Vol. 37 No. 2 (February 1986), pp. 115-122.

17. See Warren C. Ogden, John R. Arthur, and J. Martin Smith, "The Survival of Contract Terms Beyond the Expiration of a Collective Bargaining Agreement," *Labor Law Journal*, Vol. 32 No. 2 (February 1981), pp. 119-125. The case cited is *Gordon L. Raynor*, 251 NLRB 17 (1980). Also Warren C. Ogden et.al., "The Survival of Contract Terms: The Quagmire Expands," *Labor Law Journal*, Vol. 36, No. 9 (Sept. 1985), pp. 688-695.

18. *W.L. Mead Inc*, 113 NLRB 1040 (1956); *Teamsters Union Local 174 v. Lucas Flour Co.*, 369 US 95 (1962).

19. *First National Bank of Omaha*, 171 NLRB 152 (1968).

20. For a good discussion of the complexities of picketing law, see Gregory and Katz, pp. 289-340.

21. *Thornhill v. Alabama*, 310 US 88 (1940).

22. 315 US 722 (1942).

23. 336 US 490 (1949).

24. 339 US 532 (1950).

25. 345 US 192 (1953).

26. 354 US 284 (1957).

27. See the Spelfogel article cited in note 6 above for the relevant rulings with respect to picketing on private property.

28. *Sailors' Union of the Pacific (Moore Dry Dock Co.)* 92 NLRB 547 (1950).

29. *NLRB v. Denver Building and Construction Trade Council*, 341 US 675 (1951). In this case the court found an unlawful secondary boycott by finding that the general contractor was the secondary employer, with the result that the union's pressure on the general contractor to fire the subcontractor was pressure on a third party.

30. *International Union of Electrical Workers, Local 621 V. NLRB*, 366 US 667 (1961).

31. Commerce Clearing House, *Labor Law Course*, (24th Edition), p. 1711.

32. Schmidman, pp. 33-34. Also *Douds v. Metropolitan Federation of Architects*, 75 F. Supp. 672 (DC 1948).

33. *NLRB v. Truck Drivers Local 449 (Buffalo Linen Supply Co)*, 353 US 87 (1957).

34. *American Shipbuilding Co. v. NLRB*, 380 US 300 (1965).

35. *Pattern Makers' League of North America, AFL-CIO v. NLRB*, 105 S.Ct. 3064 (1985).

36. *United Steelworkers of America, AFL-CIO v. Edward Sadlowski Jr. et. al.*, 457 US 102 (1982). See the following two articles in *The Nation*, Vol. 234, No. 21 (May 29, 1982): Alan Barnes, "What Role for Outsiders," pp. 639ff, and Jules Bernstein and Lawrence E. Gold, "Should the Courts Determine Policy?" pp. 654-655.

37. This information is taken from Gordon F. Bloom and Herbert R. Northrup, *Economics of Labor Relations* (Homewood, IL: Richard D. Irwin, Inc., 1977), pp. 674-680.

38. This information is taken from Francis J. Flaherty, "Truth Technology," *The Progressive*, Vol. 46, No. 6 (June 1982), pp. 30-35; and William E. Hartsfield, "Polygraphs," *Labor Law Journal*, Vol. 36, No. 11 (November 1985), pp. 817-834.

39. *Polsky v. Radio Shack*, 666 F 2d 824 (3rd Cir., 1981).

40. See Hartsfield, pp. 819-826.

41. Jonathan A. Bennett, "Your Urine or Your Job," *The Guardian*, October 15, 1986, p. 2.

42. Virginia duRivage, "The OFCCP Under the Reagan Administration: Affirmative Action in Retreat," *Labor Law Journal*, Vol. 36, No. 6 (June 1985), pp. 360-368.

43. The case is *California Federal Savings and Loan v. Guerra*, 758 F 2d 290 (9th Cir., 1985). This quote is from Laura McClure, "Women Want Better—and Equal—Rights," *The Guardian*, (January 28, 1987) p. 2.

44. *Meritor Savings Bank v. Vinson* 106 US 2399 (1986).

45. *NLRB v. Washington Aluminum*, 370 US 9 (1962).

46. *Meyers Industries*, 268 NLRB 73 (1984).

47. See Jeremy B. Fox and Kent F. Murrmann, "NLRA Section 7 Protection in Nonunion Settings: Meyers Industries and After," *Labor Law Journal*, Vol. 37, No. 1 (January 1986), pp. 34-40.

48. For a good discussion, see Brian Hershizer, "The New Common Law of Employment: Changes in the Concept of Employment at Will," *Labor Law Journal*, Vol. 36, No. 2 (February 1985), pp. 95-107.

Notes to Chapter Six

1. Part of this section on the Labor Law Reform Bill is based upon Thomas Ferguson and Joel Rogers, "Labor Law Reform and Its Enemies," *The Nation*, Vol. 228 (January 6-13, 1979), p. 1 and pp. 17-20.

2. Thomas A. Kochan, "How American Workers View Labor Unions," *Monthly Labor Review*, Vol. 105, No. 4 (April 1979), pp. 23-31.

3. An excellent article on this whole area of anti-union organizing is "Union Busters," *Southern Exposure*, Vol. VIII, No. 2 (Summer 1980), pp. 27-48.

4. Ferguson and Rogers, p. 20.

5. Almost this entire section is based upon unpublished reports and other materials given me by Robert Baugh, former Research Director of the International Woodworkers of America.

6. Nearly all of these states became right to work states after the passage of Taft-Hartley. Only six were right to work states before June 23, 1947, when Taft-Hartley was enacted.

7. Many of the unpublished reports noted in footnote 5 above were used as the basis for the statements in this paragraph. Also see Ben-Chieh Liu, *Quality of Life Indicators in the U.S. Metropolitan Area*, 1970 (Kansas City, MO: Midwest Research Institute, 1975).

8. This quote and much of what follows are taken from a pamphlet called "Beating Right to Work," by Ken Worley, an official of the United Auto Workers.

9. See Jeremy Brecher, "Crisis Economy: Born-Again Labor Movement," *Monthly Review*, Vol. 35, No. 10 (March 1984), pp. 1-17.

_____CASE INDEX_____

(Note: The number at the end of each citation is the page on which the case is discussed in the text.)

Taracorp, 273 NLRB 54 (1984), 71, 177.

Teamsters' Union v. Vogt, Inc., 354 U.S. 284 (1957), 121.

Teamsters' Union Local 174 v. Lucas Flour Co., 369 U.S. 95 (1962), 115.

Textile Workers of America v. Darlington Manufacturing Company, 380 U.S. 263 (1965), 104.

Thornhill v. Alabama, 310 U.S. 88 (1940), 120.

United Dairy Farmers Cooperative Association v. NLRB, 633 F. 2d 1054 (3rd Cir. 1980), 98.

United Leather Workers v. Herkert & Meisel Trunk Co., 265 U.S. 457 (1924), 12-13.

United Mine Workers of America v. Coronado Coal Co., 259 U.S. 344 (1925), 13.

United Steel Workers of America, AFL-CIO v. Edward Sadlowski et. al., 457 U.S. 102 (1982), 130-131.

United Steel Workers of America v. Weber, 443 U.S. 193 (1979), 64.

United Technologies Corp., 268 NLRB 557 (1984), 103.

University of California v. Bakke, 438 U.S. 265 (1978), 63-64.

U.S. v. Brown, 381 U.S. 437 (1965), 32.

Vaca v. Sipes, 386 U.S. 171 (1967), 131.

Wendy Wygant v. Jackson Board of Education, 476 U.S. (1986), 62.

Wichita Eagle and Beacon Publishing Co., Inc. v. NLRB, 480 F. 2d 52 (10th Cir. 1973), 41.

Williams v. Saxbe, 431 F. Supp. 654 (DC Cir. 1976), 67.

SUBJECT INDEX

About South End Press

South End Press is a nonprofit, collectively run book publisher with over 150 titles in print. Since our founding in 1977, we have tried to meet the needs of readers who are exploring, or are already committed to, the politics of radical social change.

Our goal is to publish books that encourage critical thinking and constructive action on the key political, cultural, social, economic, and ecological issues shaping life in the United States and in the world. In this way, we hope to give expression to a wide diversity of democratic social movements and to provide an alternative to the products of corporate publishing.

If you would like a free catalog of South End Press books or information about our membership program—which offers two free books and a 40% discount on all titles—please write us at South End Press, 116 Saint Botolph Street, Boston, MA 02115.

Other titles of interest from South End Press:

Inside the Circle:
A Union Guide to Quality of Worklife
Mike Parker

Choosing Sides:
Unions and the Team Concept
Mike Parker

Women in the Global Factory
Annette Fuentes and Barbara Ehrenreich

Behind the Silicon Curtain:
The Seductions of Work in a Lonely Era
Dennis Hayes

Sisterhood and Solidarity:
Feminism and Labor in Modern Times
Diane Balser

Between Labor and Capital
Edited by Pat Walker

The Crisis in the Working Class:
And Some Arguments for Creating a New Labor Movement
John McDermott